PEDRO A. GONZÁLEZ JR MJ

Our Demons in the Machine
Language, Netsocities & Illiteracy on the Web

Editorial Letra Viva
Coral Gables Florida

to my sons,
to my love

Foreword

Ideologies are belief systems, which in the case of the proliferation of currents on the internet are socially shared by the immense collection of participating social actors, determined by groups and communities that spontaneously are born and grow, like cultural, professional, religious, social, or self-interest.

Hence the ideologies deployed on the Internet are fundamental social viewpoints of a relatively general and abstract nature. One of its cognitive functions is to provide ideological coherence to a group's attitudes and thus facilitate its acquisition and use in everyday situations. Among other things, ideologies also specify what values, like freedom, equality, or maybe justice, is essential to the faction.

Based on the concepts presented, ideologies, thus defined, develop perceptive and social functions such as the language of the internet and smartphones, being the basis of the discourses and other social practices of the members of social groups. That allows them to organize and coordinate their actions and interactions with a view of the group's goals and interests.

They are functioning as part of the socio-cognitive interface between the social structures of groups and their dialogs and social practices.

The purpose of the research is to determine the topicality of problems with digital illiteracy in the use of todays
and future electronic systems. A situation confronted by the
use of language, *netsocieties*, and dialogues on the Internet in general, and education in specific.

The experience of the new Pandemic, with the prevalence of interest and the use of online systems, confirms the problem of digital illiteracy in learning, not only in the students but in the administrative and academic personnel, which must confront in the middle of a crisis, the initial planning of solutions, without a complete understanding of the technology available.

The focus on the correct investment in systems and technology is part of the problem. However, the solution lies in realizing that the United States is behind internationally in learning and the proper training of the actors related to enabling the appropriate use of available technological resources.

Working on the research for this book for more than five years never prepared me to confront the experience of the Pandemic. Not that surprises me -after 45 years as a journalist, including being a War Correspondent in three continents-, a father, grandfather, and a raised as a Christian in a Communist country, it is not easy to get rattle for minor commotions.

However, it is not the use of technology. The mentality surprised academia and wasn't the moment to say: "I told you so." The resources were in the neighbor hardware shop: lights, extensions, and a new camera.

The difficulties were the intrusion of the student's intimacy, the open the door to their bedrooms, kitchens, workplaces and sometimes their cars to teach them. That's deserved a chapter on this book.

The Author

Index

INTRODUCTION

Based on how ideologies organize social attitudes, such as those related to communications, and because of their social functions, we developed a general ideological scheme defining the self-identity of groups, like norms and values, related assemblies and resources, or lack of those primary resources. (Van Dijk 2015, p. 83)

These categories explain many properties of ideologies, not entirely religious, political, or professional. However, they have ways to influence "the mental models of individual language users" (p. 64). Using the case, they need structure and representation, as other belief systems.

Thus, they are unlikely to be merely a long and messy set of beliefs, as the notion of organizing rational structures, for example, in terms of *schemata* (schemas). That is one of the main characteristics of modern cognitive psychology, as is being recognized in many theoretical studies.

The hypothesis about the organizational nature of ideologies does not imply that they are consistent. They are not logical systems, and they are socio-psycho-logical systems. So, they may be heterogeneous or incoherent, in their preliminary stages, more spontaneous, although several may try to improve coherence by explicit manifests, catechisms, or theories (p. 69)

So, while ideologies organize other social beliefs of groups, this does not mean, on the one hand, that these different social views are consistent when we also know that popular racist views argue that immigrants are lazy and do not want to work. Yet, at the same time, they occupy our workplaces.

We also know that people use various strategies to eliminate or ignore inconsistencies between ideological positions and the facts that confront them.

The emergence of the Internet can be interpreted as an informative phenomenon, changing seeing things and reality. It provides the undeniable ease of streamlining and making efficient creation, storage, and transfer of information. (Ortega Villa, 2009, p 9)

This time we will stop at a quick stop to describe them, to the Internet, as a communicative tool. If we try to define the communicative process, it will take us too long to simplify it, assimilate it and translate it into a short document.

Therefore, using a basic scheme, we will only mention that three main elements are required to conduct such a process: sender, message, and receiver.

It is important to note that while more sophisticated ways of creating and sending a message appear, complex tools and instruments for encoding-decoding information are inevitably required. Moreover, those structures have technical or technological support and relationships between objects that evolve at high speed and permanently. The Internet is no exception.

One can approach the Internet as an informative, communicative phenomenon, a catalytic tool for globalization, a catalyst of production processes, or an electronic frontier of knowledge. Although taking up the latter, currently, it is being built as a consequent and inescapable way of transferring information in large volumes. Thus, logically, knowledge at speeds unthinkable at the beginning and middle of the twentieth century, becoming subjects that participate in the knowledge society.

However, saving the ubiquity of neologisms (information society), it is already used as an accepted term, although formally, its definition is not entirely clear. Note that bureaucracies and government levels do not want to fall behind in the terminological swamps. Therefore, already the knowledge society has been mentioned.

In the so-called economic globalization, which also impacts and orientation for learning the "official" language for people's

movements and processes, is English. It also reflects this as well in the location of the contents. By obtaining results from a search for a particular topic, we
receive more information in the language of Shakespeare. (Martínez Musiño & Maya Corzo, 2004, p 3)

There is talk of a projection of the American way of life on the Internet. Scholars of the phenomena associated with the masses and cultural products dare to affirm: "Is there a process of the tendentious significance of messages or content?" (Garcia Canclini, 1993, p 38). Which leads us to ask: Will there be an intention to link edifying information, through ideological content, with global, regional, or national development? Is the Internet an enriching asset, or is it just a medium?

The media, including the Internet, have taken a leading part in disseminating culture, ideas, the construction of consciousness, and the apparent resolution of ideologies. The Internet phenomenon contains a load of information with idiomatic tendencies grouped under a lingua franca: English.

There are more significant limitations to the generation and dissemination of knowledge in languages other than English, basically determined by economic factors. The inhabitants of the planet must submit to a predominant one, English.

To the extent that we do not have a diversity of spaces for the generation, dissemination, and obtaining of information, we need to apply the principle of equity. We can say that there is an ideological discharge on those who organize, manage, and have information and communication technologies at their disposal. In this case, the Internet.

There is already a need to create a counterweight by generating information, symbols, or sets of characters that reduce uncertainty and dependence towards the hegemony of Anglo-Saxon culture.

THE SOCIAL BASIS OF IDEOLOGIES

Consequently, one of the most challenging problems has to do with the same social basis of ideologies. Assumedly they are the properties of 'social groups' and that these can be motley. However, not all social communities are 'ideological groups.' For example, passengers on a bus are not teachers at some universities.

It is, therefore, necessary to meet several social criteria on durability, continuity, social practices, interests, relationships with others. It also includes the fundamental basis of their identification: a sense of belonging to the group that would complete the human need for communication and belonging to the tribe.

In other words, all categories of performance and discourse communities are also communities, face-to-face or mediated, but communities. Ideologies are expressed and acquired through discourse, like verbal or other communicative interaction, as we see in actual communications patterns via electronic devices. Those are the terms of ideological discourse. (Tannen & Trester, 2013, p ix)

It identifies the part of the language users concerned with the situation or events that the speech deals with. That is, by its mental models. People understand a lesson if they can build a model of it, constructing and identifying the interrelationships between the components, not perfect, but workable.

The "shared" nature of knowledge in a community needs to be defined edify beyond, both cognitively and socially. (Herring, 2013, p. 1) For now, however, we make the practical decision to say that knowledge is the beliefs of a community budgeted in its public speeches addressed to the community, as is the case for most media discourses mass communication.

The most common understanding of Speech is as "text." But generically, some differences are established in the "text" as "the concrete manifestation of the discourse" that is, "the product itself"; and "discourse" as "the whole process of linguistic production that is put into play to produce something" (Gimenez, 1983, p. 125; Lozano 1997, p.p 15-16).

In theory, as a solution, let us have it in three categories: formalist (intra-discursive) approach that considers discourse as a source of itself, whether it is phrases or statements, or stories or macro-structures. (Karam, 2005)

To understand the text, we must go to the interpretative framework. In such an approach, the study may focus entirely on the syntactic (Harris, 1981) or the narrative as a story construction (Greimas & Courtés, 1982). Moreover, this perspective looks at discourse as a linguistic dimension superior to prayer, a global message, and a statement.

A second perspective, enunciative (Benveniste, 1966 & Jakobson, 1960), considers discourse a communication model. As per this view, speech refers to a particular place and time discussing specific topics of enunciation organizes its language according to a specific recipient "(you, you)."

Benveniste and Jakobson sought to unravel how the speaking subject is scribed in the statements he emits; that is, how the enunciator appears in it; how the language user appropriates it, links to it in a specific way, and records it through indexes.

Finally, the materialist perspective of Pecheux (1983) and Robin's (1973) discourse understands discourse as a social practice linked to its social conditions and framework of institutional, ideological, cultural, and historical-conjunctural production. Pecheux states that the meaning of discourse is not determined by the subject-emit but by the ideological positions within the social processes produced by it. (Karam, 2005)

Communities do not fall under the principle of determinism as their members do not always represent or express the beliefs of their groups. Ideological discourse is personally and contextually variable. (Van Dijk, 2008, p. viii) arriving at the politically 'correct' or 'incorrect' discourse as a challenge of social positions.

Usually, when analyzing language, it is classified into verbal and non-verbal. The first is the most widely studied and known by people, both in a formal and explored context or in daily life, in reading, writing, and face-to-face communication. We often forget that non-verbal aspects also transmit information and decoding; this does not require some training since it corresponds to a social construction constituted in practice. (Gabriel, 2017)

Nonetheless, the current century has found a third variant of the language, referring to the forms of computer-mediated communication, which take place in a new arena - the virtual - and with new ways in which participants seize it. Studying these modifications has been an object of great interest for scholars from various theoretical fields since the emergence of electronic devices used for interpersonal communication (Herring, 2008).

One of the most striking aspects is using EMOJIS [1] , originally sequences of punctuation marks that, rotated 90°, schematically represented facial expressions. (Such, 2016)

---

[1] Emoticon usage in English with the Japanese version, *kaomoji*: "face-marks". (Markman, 2007, p 3)

"Unless one denies the cognitive nature of meaning and understanding, any empirical definition of discourse involves cognitive notions of some kind." (Van Dijk, 2006, p. 133) Meaning the act or process of knowing, perceiving, relating to the mental processes of perception, memory, judgment, and reasoning, as contrasted with emotional and volitional processes, as the dictionary reflects. (Cognitive, 2019)

Ideologies, as a rule, appear in discourse through their underlying structures, such as polarization between the positive description of the endogenous group and the negative description of the exogenous one. As in social media online behavior, political messages can be "echo chambers" to fuel polarization. (Iyengar et al., 2019, p. 130)

Page et al. (2014) define social media as "the Internet-based sites and services that promote social interaction between participants." (p 5)

Looks simplistic? They differentiate it from mass media, a 'broadcasting mechanism' as a free for all that as a 'social umbrella' group together forms and genres, with a given amplitude of space from sales to multicolor opinions that -like us humans do- go from madness to brilliance. (p 6)

It is possible to achieve this objective without resorting to a propositional approach by employing themes, meanings, or other means, such as lexicalization, syntactic structure, or semantic movements. You can also achieve this by making many claims and featuring many figures of speech.

Thus, we can observe the influence of ideological 'prejudice' of mental models and underlying social representations based on ideologies at all levels of text and speech. Despite the ideological control of some discourse structures, not all of them are, and that no configuration of the speech has ideological functions only.

It all depends on the context, defined here as the subjective mental models -which can themselves be ideological- that represent relevant properties of communicative situations.

The dispute over the nature of language on the internet is evident in the numerous nomenclatures that researchers have proposed to try to account for the novel characteristics of linguistic use in digital environments. One of the first definitions is interactive written discourse, 'interactive written speech.'

We now can claim that by rendering the dominant form of media contents as speech-like and interactive writing, the internet supports the birth of a community-like social organization surrounding us, all around the world, or, in the brilliant words of Marshal McLuhan's, a 'global village' (1970, p. 41):

"[The] visual, specialist and fragmented Westerner have now to live in closest daily association with all the ancient oral cultures of the Earth, but [also] his own electric technology now begins to translate the visual or eye man back into the tribal and the oral pattern with its seamless web of kinship and interdependence." (McLuhan 1964, p. 50)

The bridge between orality and writing becomes an 'oralized written text,' an expression very suitable for chats, subject to a process of "channeling" of written discourse. Social networks resulted in the right to public speaking, dominating spaces it did not occupy in the past due to computer-mediated communication, with the ability to respond effectively to the discourses received.

Immediacy, low editing and censorship, anonymity, and non-traceability are characteristics of these impulses:

"Thanks to interactive technology, ordinary audiences are now able to produce written and visual responses to the messages they receive. These responses can spread and possess high symbolic capital, heralding a new age that we may dub "the age of audience response." (Latif, 2017, p. 292)

Bolander and Locher recapitulate opinions from different authors, and they present their theory as:

"Scholars working with computer-mediated data in their study of language use online are confronted with a striking amount of diversity. Researchers nowadays recognise that there is no such thing as a monolithic variety of Internet language. Rather, language online is varied and CMC[2] practices are changing fast. Based on Hymes' (1974)[3] SPEAKING mnemonic, a framework guiding research conducted within an "ethnography of speaking" tradition, Herring (2007)[4] succinctly summarises the diversity of computer-mediated data according to ten "medium factors" and eight "social factors". Her so-called "faceted classification scheme for computer-mediated discourse" can be used as a methodological tool for researchers wishing to study language use in computer-mediated environments, as each of the factors listed in her scheme has been shown to influence language use online. Yet it can also be seen as a descriptive framework which makes manifest the diverse properties of computer-mediated data." (2014, p 15).

---

[2] Comptuter-Mediated Communication,
[3] Refers to Hymes, D., 2013. Foundations in sociolinguistics: An ethnographic approach. Routledge.
[4] Refers to Herring, Susan C. 2007. A faceted classification scheme for computer-mediated discourse. Language@internet 4.

Conative or appellative language dominates social media outlets like Facebook. The predominant element is the receiver, and the communicative intention influences it through instructions, advice, and questions.

There are many exhortative and interrogative statements, imperative and indicative statements, second-person verbal statements, and vocative statements. (Mancera Rueda & Pano Alamán, p 308)

People play with language, dispensing with normative spelling and grammar to a certain extent. Young people may use non-normative words for varied reasons, such as the comfort or speed of writing. That is, by the poor planning in the elaboration of the discourse, other phenomena may be due to factors of a pragmatic nature, such as the desire to attract the interlocutor's attention or to configure one's identity differentiating oneself from others.

Finally, Twitter is a microblogging or nano blogging platform, an online service that allows you to send and publish messages of no more than 140 characters. In this channel, messages have different communicative functions (Tíscar Lara, 2012).

Meaning recognition, when the texts of others are retweeted, and their authority over the information shared is recognized; dialogic, which allows you to converse with someone by inserting "@user" in the message or simply by clicking on the Reply button.

By incorporating tags, discourse facilitates the follow-up of different tweets on the same topic; and identity because in the user's profile appear photographs and a brief description that identify him. (Mancera Rueda & Pano Alamán, p 308)

GOING BACK TO THE THEORY

As Professors Peter A. Michalove, Stefan Georg, and Alexis Manaster Ramer wrote:

"The genealogical classification of languages has been the subject of investigation for more than two centuries, and progress continues to be made in deepening our understanding of language change, both in theoretical terms and in the study of specific language families. In recent years. as in the past, many new proposals of linguistic relationships have been constructed. Some promising to various degrees and others clearly untenable. The debate about specific recent proposals is part of the healthy process needed to evaluate proposed relationships. discard those that prove incorrect. and refine those of merit. Rather than evaluating the relative linguistic "distance" between potentially related languages, with temporal distance leading to some point where we cannot distinguish real relationships from chance similarities, we propose a scale of easy to difficult relationships in which temporal distance is only one factor that makes some relationships more recognizable than others." (Michalove et al., 1998, p. 451)

Different technical and socio-cultural changes justify this need to overcome the previous approaches and integrate new methods. A study from the UK University of Oxford highlights the increasing internet penetration, the current patterns of a permanent connection, blending between fundamental and digital, and technological changes.

Among these, it is worth noting the increasing introduction and circulation of different semiotic products, such as written text, images, audios, and videos, a perspective of studies that proposes the consideration of extra semiotic resources in the study of communication and representation (Adami, 2016, p. 453).

"Written communication in instant messaging, text messaging, chat, and other forms of electronic communication appears to have generated a "new language" of abbreviations, acronyms, word combinations, and punctuation. In this naturalistic study, adolescents, collected their instant messaging conversa-
tions for one week and then completed a spelling test delivered over instant messaging. We used the conversations to develop a taxonomy of new language use in instant messaging. Short-cuts, including abbreviations, acronyms, and unique spellings were most prevalent in the instant message conversation, followed by pragmatic signals, such use of emoticons, emotion words, and punctuation, and typographical and spelling errors were uncommon. With rare exceptions, notably true spelling errors, spelling ability was not related to use of new language in instant messaging. The taxonomy provides an important tool for investigating new language use and the results provide partial evidence that new language does not have a harmful effect on conventional written language." (Varnhagen et al., 2010, p. 719)

El Ouirdi et al. (2014) tried to define 'what are social media, applying the 'Laswellian framework'[5] and they concluded that:

"New social media platforms are constantly emerging, making

[5] Harold Hasswell (1902-1978) model of communication appear in an article called *The Structure and Function of Communication in Society*, organizing "scientific study of the process of communication." (Haswell, 1948, p 216)

it a challenge to keep up with the fastpaced evolution in the field. The provided definition and taxonomy of social media will hopefully help managers have a clearer visualization of existing social media platforms and assist researchers in identifying new ve
ues for research." (p 123)

Semiotics describes communication processes, not in terms of message exchange, but in meaning production, sign action, semiosis, meaning production processes, meaning systems, cultural processes of symbolic interactions.

These expand the space of relevance not only of the object "communication" but also of its ontological nature, epistemological and phenomenal.

From the semiotic point of view, the transmission not only appears as the emission and reception of messages but does not necessarily appear linked to the mass media. It also appears as something else, as a constructive element and generator of structurally both at the biological and social levels. (Vidales Gonzáles, p 39)

Interaction appears as a building concept or a dynamizing element in semiotic systems when the mathematic theory of information applies. Semiotics infers that it has not dialogued with media studies or with the production of theoretical principles within these studies. Still, it has dialogued with the mathematical proposal and its subsequent developments, as is the case of cybernetics. (Pierce & Corey, 2009, p 184)

In a contemporary movement, communication has moved to the center of reflection in the semiotic space; therefore, if semiotics has used it as a constructive element.

It is not a specific or predetermined relationship between it and interaction study. A research program also emphasizes the centrality of semiosis and communication in the organization and development of living organisms, societies, cultures, and the circulation of meanings.

How does language become from Technological a human discourse?

It is impossible to think about technological advances without considering their impact on society and its interactions. Digital platforms have opened a world of possibilities for different human activities. Still, they also present several human interaction limitations that give rise to new needs, communicative and social.

For this purpose, discuss a commonality; there must be similar codes. The academic field of communication refers to this from the mathematical model introduced by Claude E. Shannon and Weaver in 1949. Contemporary works repeatedly address this theme from various perspectives. (Floridi, 2019)

> "The word information relates not so much to what you do say, as to what you could say. The mathematical theory of communication deals with the carriers of information, symbols and signals, not with information itself. That is, information is the measure of your freedom of choice when you select a message" (Shannon & Weaver, 1949, p. 12).

The transmission of information through telecommunications equipment has evolved and formed an essential part of our daily lives. We went from the telegraph to WhatsApp and from black and white television, which deserved its own space, to high-resolution portable cell phones or tablets that can be taken to the bathroom. (Soto Delgado, 2021)

But technological devices provide a practical value and aesthetic and symbolic that lead us to choose between an endless number of options: not only the most efficient but the most beautiful, the best design, or the one that gives me the most significant status.

(Licona, 2018)

It is worthwhile then to start reflecting on technology in our daily lives by questioning how to use it and why and for what.

Well-applied technology helps us, for example: to organize ourselves better, to learn new things, to keep track of our goals and personal advances, or to shorten distances with friends or family. However, the other side of the coin is that we can be bombarded with harmful, stressful information or seek out situations in which we are at risk.

Universities register increased cases of depression and anxiety linked to the use of social networks. (Ahmad, 2019)

On social media, we interact and exchange information with people with whom we somehow have something in common, filtering the things we upload or remove from our profiles based on the number of LIKES, SHARES, or COMMENTS we receive.

This "attention economy" depends entirely on the reaction that provokes the interest of others and their responses on social networks. Studies have found that each like generates dopamine production in the brain and activates reward-linked systems, so they are so addictive. (Ahmad, 2019)

A good dose of likes and exchanges can make us feel excellent and contribute to our self-esteem. The problem comes when there is nothing to support my self-esteem and my links; therefore, the issue with social networks, technology, and the mind, has nothing to do with isolating us and depriving us of the exchange, but in landing how we use them.

We need to realize that we tend to see people's achievements in the networks. The most significant likes come in the face of success and exceptional situations. Hence, the more people post about these times. The less they post about their daily moments of doubt, anxiety, or failure. Keeping this in mind is essential since depressive disorders linked to social networks compare our lives and everyday moments with others without considering unique issues.

(Generación Anahuac, 2019 & Admin, 2020)

As Joseph A. Paradiso, from MIT Media Lab, wrote:

"The Internet of Things starts from the premise of the ubiquity of environments equipped with sensors. Without the sensors, the cognitive engines of this world, full of active devices, would be blind, deaf and dumb and would not be able to give a relevant response to the real-world events they intend to increase. The last decade has seen endless advances, thanks to the way sensors tend to take advantage of Moore's law. In this sense, there seems to be a growing proliferation of sensors of all kinds and everywhere, indicating an imminent transition phase when they are well connected in the network, just as we witnessed a fundamental change in our interaction with computers when web search engines appeared. This change will create a continuous electronic nervous system that will cover the planet. Therefore, one of the main challenges of today's computational community lies in how to integrate this "omniscient" and rapidly evolving sensor system into human perception. " (p 48)

Community destiny, target communities, here is the 'brand' of tribalism: "They do not gather people around something rational but around non-rational elements." (Maffesoli, 1996, p. 69) For him, "the community if destiny is an accommodation to the natural and social environment, and as such is forced to confront heterogeneity in its various guises." (p. 126)

These needs have resulted in various solutions or trends in the digital language, such as contractions, the preponderance of visual elements in communication — understood emoticons or emojis — and the adoption of cultural symbols to convey messages, known as memes. Every meme has several senses and social functions. (Pérez Salazar et al., 2014, p 84)

The term meme, initially, is linked to the area of biology. In fact, in 1976, the evolutionary scientist Richard Dawkins in his book *The Selfish Gene* recorded the concept:

"The new soup is the soup of human culture. We need a name for the new replicator, a noun that conveys the idea of a unit of cultural transmission or a unit of imitation. 'Mimeme' comes from a suitable Greek root, but I want a monosyllable that sounds a bit like 'gene.' I hope my classicist friends will forgive me if I abbreviate mimeme to meme. If it is any consolation, it could alternatively be thought of as being related to 'memory', or to the French word meme. It should be pronounced to rhyme with 'cream.'" (Dawkins, 2006, p. 249)

The study of viral propagation images or content, known as memes, has been studied from memetics, proposed by Richard

Dawkins (2006) and Susan Blackmore (2000). The main element - the meme- is transmitted from one consciousness to another, varying slightly, by imitation and with three characteristics: fidelity, fertility, and longevity. Following the meme-as-virus analogy sees a similarity between them and disease agents. (Shifman, 2013, p. 365)

As Dawkins's definition presents the meme as an individual unit, independent or context-related, this is the previously most used or accepted definition; however, recent authors have begun to understand the meme as part of

a system, a dependent or context-related entity. (Canizzaro, 2016, p. 571)

Why are memes so crucial in digital language? We could say those memes as a set of cultural elements and take advantage of all the possibilities of digital platforms — combining text, images, and video in different forms. They are the epitome of its evolution, efficiently summarizing previous information or knowledge to convey something new.

As Elena Álvarez Mellado in the Spanish newspaper, *El Diario* [The Daily] wrote:

"Memes, on the other hand, are inherently colloquial and therefore live outside the walls of all formality,
that is, outside the jurisdiction of the RAE[6]. One may want to compose a formal WhatsApp message, but aspiring to generate a "formal meme" (whatever that is) seems like a contradiction in terms. In fact, a walk-through social networks is enough to verify that deliberate spelling transgression is actually one of the hallmarks of memes in particular and of the language of the internet in general: "baia, baia", "haber si me muero", "berdadera hizquierda", "halluda"... Social networks (and especially Twitter), are full of linguistic uses capable of

---

[6] Royal Spanish Academy for the Spanish Language, the official institution for the stability of the language.

making purists unfamiliar with internet speech cry blood." (2018)[7]

One of the answers that seek to support the phenomenon of memes is the digitization of information and the interactivity of new media. Since these facilitate the creation and subsequent dissemination of content, thus generating a user who not only consumes but also produces and/or edits material (Arango, 2015, p.9).

Also, you no longer need to be a university professional (graphic designer, illustrator, publicist, among others) or an artist to create a work that contains a message that several people see. You only need a computer with an in-access. Furthermore, it is not even necessary to buy the respective editing programs since there are now free versions online and websites that fulfill the same function (Veléz, 2015, p.2).

Young people do not use memes outside the internet to communicate. Or it is failing that, the use of memes in specific social media platforms such as WhatsApp, Twitter, and Facebook. It is also unknown if memes can be distinguished from emoticons or emojis. (Bustos Reyes, 2016, p 7)

---

[7] Original in Spanish: Los memes, en cambio, son inherentemente coloquiales y viven, por tanto, extramuros de toda formalidad, es decir, fuera de la jurisdicción de la RAE. Uno puede querer redactar un mensaje de whatsApp formal, pero aspirar a generar un "meme formal" (sea lo que sea eso) parece una contradicción en términos. De hecho, basta un paseo por las redes sociales para comprobar que la transgresión ortográfica deliberada es en realidad una de las señas de identidad de los memes en particular y de lengua de internet en general: "baia, baia", "haber si me muero", "berdadera hizquierda", "halluda"... Las redes sociales (y muy especialmente Twitter), están cuajadas de usos lingüísticos capaces de hacer llorar sangre a los puristas poco familiarizados con el habla de internet.

ANIMALS WITH EMOTIONS

The human being is a primarily social animal, which has based much of its evolution and progress on language, which feeds back the perception of the reality of societies. Human activity, from the technologies used daily, gives rise to new codes and programming languages, a new jargon within different digital platforms, and the viralization of memes or macro images.

A new digital language has begun to emerge, answering the need for a common one to allow us to understand the reality on a global scale and cooperate, learn, and build knowledge between cultures with a previously different form of speech.

Aristotle suggested that abstraction or introspection was an essential part of the cognitive process, the highest. For his part, the German philosopher George Hegel (1770-1831) defined abstract-universal representation through an image depending on the sensitivity of its content.

Therefore, they can observe the degree of representativeness that an image possesses through how the content affects the recipient emotionally and intellectually. (Thomas, 2014)

As Dr. Josiah Royce puts Hegel's essential insight: "I know myself only in so far as I am known or may be known by another than my present or momentary self." (Royce, 1892, p. 207)

Thus, according to Hegel's Logic (Encyclopedia of the Philosophical Sciences, 1830), language is the element that draws persons out of their subjectivity into a unity that reveals their universal nature. (Nicolacopoulos & Vassilacopoulos, 2005, p. 18)

Because Aristotle confirmed that we faced daily a few years ago, we need the rest to survive physiologically, intellectually, and emotionally. These conditions are all aspects of our lives.

Aristotle has already pointed out that "what differentiates man from other animals is the word" and that this ability to express ourselves is the vehicle for articulating society. Thus, this need for communication explains phenomena or less the irruption of social platforms -like *Facebook, Twitter, YouTube, Instagram*- in our daily lives.

This rise of social networks leaves a digital footprint that collects our uses, customs, interests, opinions, tastes, etc. Hence, the more negligible inconvenience that analyzing them becomes a titanic task if you do not have the right tools. This need has given new impetus to another type of chameleonic-looking animal, which we now call "data science."

Currently, we have microscopes to study society from different angles and with various levels of detail or zoom. In the case of natural language processing techniques, we can both break down what is said on social networks and get to know the linguistic profile of a criminal. For example, we can use free tools to compare the last two Christmas speeches with little effort.

Now, extracting meaning from the conversation requires platforms like Lynguo that categorize and analyze feelings, emotions, or even awareness. In addition, advances in computational linguistics will enable us to accurately explore the conversation on social networks. However, it is also true that it is not yet possible to properly treat metaphors or irony.

If we increase the zoom of the microscope, we can go beyond the global conversation and focus on the conversations that occur between groups of users. The first step is to draw the interaction maps, detailed **who mentions or retweets whom** on Twitter. Then, you can extract collective dialogs from them, as we did, for example, during the Ebola crisis.

Xiangkuabg Zhang et al. (2021) published this year a study titled: *Rise and fall of the global conversation and shifting sentiments during the COVID-19*:

"Social media (e.g., Twitter) has been an extremely popular tool for public health surveillance. The novel coronavirus disease 2019 (COVID-19) is the first pandemic experienced by a world connected through the internet. We analyzed 105+ million tweets collected between March 1 and May 15, 2020, and Weibo messages compiled between January 20 and May 15, 2020, covering six languages (English, Spanish, Arabic, French, Italian, and Chinese) and represented an estimated 2.4 billion citizens worldwide. To examine fine-grained emotions during a pandemic, we built machine learning classification models based on deep learning language models to identify emotions in social media conversations about COVID-19, including positive expressions (optimistic, thankful, and empathetic), negative expressions (pessimistic, anxious, sad, annoyed, and denial), and a complicated expression, joking, which has not been explored before. Our analysis indicates a rapid increase and a slow decline in the volume of social media conversations regarding the pandemic in all six languages. The upsurge was triggered by a combination of economic collapse and confinement measures across the regions to which all the six languages belonged except for Chinese, where only the latter drove conversations. Tweets in all analyzed languages conveyed remarkably similar emotional states as the epidemic was elevated to pandemic status, including feelings dominated by a mixture of joking with anxious/pessimistic/annoyed as the volume of conversation surged and shifted to a general increase in positive states (optimistic, thankful, and empathetic), the strongest being expressed in Arabic tweets, as the pandemic came under control." (p 1)

These groups encompass users who talk more to each other than each other. Each one acts as a microcosm with its dynamics, which generate *trending topics,* local **in**fluencers, users who act as a bridge between the different groups. A curiosity, this conversation always appears differentiated when it comes to political issues. (Hague, 2020)

By moving from general to a cluster and then to individuals, then to customers, we can also see how their friends and family influence their purchasing decisions or how to detect business opportunities and improve their experiences as customers based on what they share on social networks.

And, beyond public social media, we can also take our microscope within organizations to understand how they work internally. Thus, we can measure effective collaboration and draw the non-formal organizational chart based on how employees relate.

In short, to measure the social behavior of these "animals" with which we live, we only need a suitable microscope. It is challenging to choose the lens well and know how to focus on it. The fact that one can discover more than one might think is even more relevant now than ever, "we are masters of our silences and slaves of our words."[8] (Cortés, 2006)

---

[8] Old arab proverb

LANGUAGE AND MEN (OR WOMEN)

It is almost impossible to separate man from language from the moment of birth to the last day of our lives; this is the medium through which we establish and maintain our most significant human relationships while serving as an instrument for carrying out the most daily transactions. (Gumperz & Cook-Gumperz, 1997, p. 5).

In this way, the value of language lies in its versatility, both in its ability to facilitate mundane tasks and provide meaning. As we delve into the particularities of how language works, we discover details of our humanity—describing man and language results in describing the same thing.

Great thinkers have already expressed it in various ways, such as Octavio Paz, noting that "the word is the man itself"[9] (Paz, 1972, p. 8) or Scott Soames in describing the central feature of language is "how represents the world" (Soames, 2010, p. 8) is a "vehicle for expressing one's thoughts, rather than a social institution participation in which extends one's cognitive reach." (p. 30)

Beyond merely being a cultural creation, Language has become a way of distinguishing and understanding the
human being, its relationships, and its social and cognitive evolution.

Just look at the works of philosophers in history as examples of the relevance of language when reflecting on human nature. (Crowell, 2017)

Any communicative activity depends on a system of

---

[9] Original in Spanish "La palabra es el hombre mismo. Estamos hechos de palabras. Ellas son nuestra única realidad o, al menos, el único testimonio de nuestra realidad. No hay pensamiento sin lenguaje, ni tampoco objeto de conocimiento: lo primero que hace el hombre frente a una realidad desconocida es nombrarla, bautizarla". *El Arco y la Lira* (Paz, 1972, p. 6)

significance that, at least minimally, participants (both biological and symbolic) must share. These signals are produced, perceived, and subsequently recognized within that system of significance that gives them meaning.

The communication process is also shared, shared space, interjective, so its significance is shaped by pre-existing conventions or meanings, which serve as a mold for the representations through which perception, purpose, and knowledge are created and structured. (Romeu Aldaya, 2013, p. 126)

Bateson categorizes animal interaction as iconic, with direct relationships between messages and signals, while giving the human language the category of digital, with messages built from different elements, resulting in relationships between signs and completely arbitrary messages.

The lyrics and vowels are only sounds devoid of meaning. By uniting them and arbitrary combinations, the sense is achieved, dependent on a previous universe of knowledge. Grammar is essential as a universe of rules that gives meaning to each language or dialect.

However, the developed language, as a characteristic of humanity, evolves with technology because "social group communications can be explained as learned coordinating signals without 'speakers' knowing why they are acting as they are." (Pagel, 2017, p. 1) Paralleling biological evolution as fast as new 'tech' with 'natural selection' of words and images.[10] (Darwin, 1889, p.59-60)

As Mark Pagel (2017) wrote:

"Possessing language, then, is behind humans' ability to produce sophisticated cultural adaptations that have

---

[10] "I may take this opportunity of remarking that my critics frequently assume that I attribute all changes of corporeal structure and mental power exclusively to the natural selection of such variations as are often called spontaneous; whereas, even in the first edition of the 'Origin of Species' I distinctly stated that great weight must be attributed to the inherited effects of use and disuse, with respect both to the body and mind". (Darwin, 1889, p. iv)

accumulated one on top of the other throughout our history as a species. Today because of this capability we live in a world full of technologies that few of us even understand. Because culture, riding on the back of language, can evolve more rapidly than genes, the relative genetic homogeneity of humanity in contrast to our cultural diversity shows that our 'aural DNA' has probably been more important in our short history than genes." (p 5)

Technological advancement has resulted in an unprecedented rapprochement between cultures and human groups and endless opportunities for communication. It has allowed for new transactions and efficient or facilitated others. It is to be hoped that unique social and linguistic needs will also emerge with these new conditions and possibilities.

It is possible to mention writing, going to the printing press, telegram, radio, and television, each improving the levels of communication expressed from its limitations. From the telegraph to the 'spurt' in social networking sites, becoming "a convention of the online landscape" (Baruah, 2012, p. 4) from sites, like *MySpace* (who started in 2003), *LinkedIn* (2003), *Facebook* (2004) and *Twitter* (2006).

In other sense, blogs, with free building tools like *Wordpress.com*, *Blogspot.com*, and *Blogger.com*, or content generating and sharing: Photo-sharing sites *Flicker.com, picasaweb. google.com*, video sharing sites like *youtube.com*, slide sharing sites like *slideshare.com*, document: *docstoc.com,* and finally sharing sites like docstoc.com. (Dowerah Baruah, 2012, p 4)

Some of the ones not mentioned frequently are the 'user appraisal sites,' like www.mouthshut.com or www. pagalguy.com, which serve as a starting point of consumer's decision-making model for gathering information about products or services they are contemplating buying as sources of information. (p. 4)

Due to the rise of electronics and microchips and the growing importance of telecommunications and Internet development, the present era has evolved into today. Due to the constraints presented by the digital space, language has also been adapted and modified in response to this change.

The nature of digital and the Internet seem to differ from author to author; however, some keywords are constant in the works around these concepts. Dr. Heather Brooke_(2016) described the digital revolution using terms such as 'transparency,' 'communicative abundance' -citing the lecture of Professor John Keane (Keane, 2011, p. 2)- and 'global interconnection.' (Brooke, 2016, p. 1)

On the other hand, Lee Rainie and Barry Wellman, in their book *Networked: The New Social Operating System* (2012), mostly use the word 'connectivity' and elaborate the term 'networked individualism' (Rainie & Wellman, 2012, p. 19) They refer to the revolution that is currently manifesting itself.

Simon J. Bronner (2011) wrote about it:

"The Internet has not displaced tradition but instead given rise to digital forms of folklore. A user-oriented folk Web may be said to active, especially among youth, that is often framed to subvert or counter a corporate, official Internet. A revision of the "analog" or relational definition of folklore in favour of a "digital" or analytical concept focusing on the variable repetition of practices. A comparison is given of folkloric transmission in analog and digital conduits with the lore of Budd Dwyer who committed suicide in 1987. In this example and folk speech evident in cyberculture, the implication is that the practice of the folk Web is comparable to latrinalia, which suggests a projection of naturalistic feces play in response to the anxiety of being controlled by a corporate, official technology." (p 32)

José van Dijck (Professor Johanna Francisca Theodora Maria 'José' Van Dijck), in various of her texts on the digital world and social networks, frequently addresses terms such as 'openness,' 'connectivity' and the use of social platforms for "mobilization and communication purposes." (Poell & Van Dijck, 2015, p. 527)

It is precisely the emergence of these new forms and trends mentioned by Padilla that represent the emergence of a particular language within the digital world, in this case, speech has been particularly affected by revolutions earlier because, as mentioned above and as the following postulate of David Crystal explains "Language is at the heart of the Internet, for Net activity is interactivity. The

Net is a system which links together a vast number of computers and the people who use them." (Crystal, 2004, p. 237), citing John Naughton[11] (1999, p. 40).

Determining where the linguistic evolution will continue is as complicated as deciding which new gadget will hit the market to revolutionize the technology sector.

Language is one more tool that human beings have used to develop their social capacities and accelerate their evolutionary process as a species. Moreover, the technological revolution has implied a particular impulse to language, changing the ways of understanding how communication works.

There is no doubt that this generates uncertainty and raises many questions regarding what we know so far. However, to close oneself to the idea that our way of relating to others is evolving would be to deny the human nature constantly changing to achieve new goals. (Esparza Hernández & Padierna Beltrán, 2018, p 80)

Understanding the digital environment and its evolution will also make it possible to foresee– to some extent – where language will evolve and what new forms of expression will emerge.

---

[11] "The community of users came up with a new conception of what 'networking' meant – not so much the sharing of machines as the linking of people." (Naughton, 2016, p. 8)

Understanding the emergence of this own form of communication involves knowing the characteristics of the medium, which has guided users to adapt to previous forms of interaction and develop new ones to solve their needs. As some authors called, we are generations of "virtual needs," in the daily ritual of "building connections between people that ultimately leads to higher satisfaction and higher loyalty to the social platform." (Krishen et al., 2016, p. 5249)

"Digitization democratizes information and values all binary units as equal, either 0 or 1, regardless of the significant symbol systems they represent, such as text, speech, or icons. The developer can create data classes, where an image can inherit characteristics from the text. This technique makes data manipulation highly efficient." (Newhagen & Rafaeli, 1996, p. 5)

Another of the qualities mentioned by the authors that it is possible to exemplify is physical distance and lack of nonverbal communication. We must not forget that digital messages are transmitted through mediators that are electronic devices. In this sense, there is no longer a face-to-face conversation but a monitor to monitor.

Similarly, other levels of interaction, such as voice with its tone or speed, are absent in several digital conversations. However, virtual deployments such as social networks have implemented media that add to these lost levels, such as voice notes or video calls. Complementing this lack of physical contact and verbal communication is the lack of written one.

An additional element to consider in understanding language

modification in digital discourse is the global thing of the medium, which relates to its interactivity. Alternatively, as Dr. Jannis Androutsopoulos called: 'digital networked writing,' or "Public discourse sometimes raises the effects of digital media on 'a language' as a whole." (Androutsopoulos, 2011, p. 2)

As Blitvich and Bou-Franch (2018) put it:

"The analysis of digital discourse lies at the intersection of (non) language resources, society and technology. Therefore, digital researchers can draw on a range of diverse socially-oriented language disciplines, whose methods and research tools may be of use in carrying out empirical research. However, some of these methods and tools may need to be critically assessed and reflectively adapted, and perhaps also expanded and even combined with others to suitably account for the communicative practices that occur in the digital world and their embeddedness within the social world at large. Discourse, in our view, is concerned with "social practice" [Fairclough, 1992, p. 28][12] rather than language in use, as it was originally – and more narrowly – conceived in 1980s-1990s. Therefore, we view discourse analysis as the study of "the ways people build and manage their social world using various semiotic systems" [Jones, Chik &, Hafner, 2015, p 3][13]. Put differently, in our view, digital discourse analysis is concerned with how multimodal, multisemiotic resources are employed to enact identities, activities and ideologies in the digital world, as part of a larger social world [Gee, 2005][14]." (p. 4)

---

[12] Reffers to Fairclough, N. (1992). Discourse and social change. Cambridge: Polity Press.
[13] Reffers to Jones, R. H., Chik, A., & Hafner, C. A. (2015). Introduction: Discourse analysis and digital practices. In R. H. Jones, A. Chik, & C. A. Hafner (Eds.), Discourse analysis and digital practices: Doing discourse analysis in the digital age (pp. 1- 17). London: Routledge
[14] Gee, J. P. (2005). An introduction to discourse analysis: Theory and method. London: Routledge.

American essayist Sven Birkerts is amazed at "how enthusiastically we are adopting our recent technologies, all without exception" and warns that "if you suggest that these choices are changing us and our world severely, you will be met with misunderstanding and irritation" (Birkerts, 2015).

The words chosen to announce the novelties ("progress" or "improvement") convey a very concrete ideology in which renewal and the ephemeral, even more so in everything related to consumption, are fundamentally sound. One even reaches "technological determinism" (Rendueles, 2013), which is nothing but faith that technological changes will bring about a better world in a naïve update of the classic Deus ex Machina. (Alcántara-Plá, 2016)

The overall presentation of modern technologies as guarantors of a better democracy is a sample. It has been insisted ad nauseam on the critical role that social networks had had in the indignant movements of the last decade, like Occupy Wall Street, 15M, Arab Spring, etc. It happened long before there were scientific studies that recognized or denied this relevance. For the moment, these make us lean more towards the latter (Fuchs, 2014).

Due to their intense incorporation into our language and our lives. It allows analyzing discursive aspects that can help us better understand how electronic innovations (and the new terminology they bring with them) affect our societies beyond superficial, optimistic, or
affect our societies beyond superficial, optimistic, or catastrophic readings, to which we are accustomed. (Alcántara-Plá, 2016)

This complexity explains why Robert P. Worden has pointed out a parallel between the evolution of words and the concept "meme" of Richard Dawkins (Worden, 2000). It is a cultural heritage unit, like genes, and naturally selected thanks to its survival's "phenotypic" consequences in a particular setting (Dawkins, 1976).

What makes words a type of meme is that they contain the information provided by their experiences and transmitted from generation to generation culturally. When the scope changes, the term can also do so as an adaptation.

Suppose we use an existing word for a new meaning, as with many terms in recent technologies. In that case, we usually do so because both concepts, the current and the incorporated, have standard features that allow us to connect metaphorically. For example, we now use "cloud" to refer to the Internet servers where we store our documents. Thanks to the reality that in our imagination, the Network is located physically on us (that is why we "upload" files to it and "download" them from it).

In the same way, we call the data entry peripheral "mouse" because it is the size of these rodents and has a shape that remembers them. Thus, it is evident that most of the features of a meteorological cloud and an Internet server are not coincident -neither those of the peripheral and the rodent.

However, this does not prevent the metaphor from working communicatively and has become conventionalized.

The exciting thing for our study is that all traits, expected or not, come to share a common conceptual space in the word's meaning (Grady et al., 1999; Croft & Cruse, 2004).

Returning to the example of the cloud, although traits such as being innocuous or positive are not part of the characteristics that allow the union of both concepts, they are incorporated into the symbolic meaning once the connection has occurred. If we call a server a "cloud," it's hard for us to think of it in terms of violence, intense colors, or pollution. If we call a device a "mouse," we do not consider it vital or justify a high price.

Being a technology that connects multiple users simultaneously requires a language that allows more remarkable universality and shared symbolic content. Having the same type of symbols promotes digital conversation and interactions between users, the key to social innovation, not only with technology but with "new ways of thinking and doing." (Murray et al., 2010, p. 38)

Language has required finding ways to achieve near-universality. No matter what cultures, languages, and geography—the latter particularly marked as missing in the digital world—messages can be encoded and decoded. Alternatives have emerged, focused on 'universal' emotions and gestures that are represented to be used across platforms.

As Linda Light (2017) considered:

"All human languages are symbolic systems that make use of symbols to convey meaning. A **symbol** is anything that serves to refer to something else but has a meaning that cannot be guessed because there is no obvious connection between the symbol and its referent. This feature of human language is called arbitrariness. For example, many cultures assign meanings to certain colors, but the meaning for a particular color may be completely different from one culture to another. Western cultures like the United States use the color black to represent death, but in China it is the color white that symbolizes death. White in the United States symbolizes purity and is used for brides' dresses, but no Chinese woman would ever wear white to her wedding. Instead, she usually wears red, the color of good luck. Words in languages are symbolic in the same way. The word *key* in English is pronounced exactly the same as the word *qui* in French, meaning "who," and *ki* in Japanese, meaning "tree." One must learn the language in order to know what any word means." (p 82)

It would be a mistake to say that the human factor is being lost. What needs to be talked about is not a loss but a modification. It could be said that digital language is the adaptation of the standard language to take advantage of opportunities and cope with the constraints of digital platforms.

It also refers to developing a standard symbology of community members that may or may not share a common geographic location or traditional language.

The construction of the tools for decoding these symbols, concerning their context and their particular use, has several supporting pillars.

The first is the global context of globalization, where the forms of expression of the Western world (mostly) are common among young people from specific social sectors.

Secondly, the massification of certain socio-cultural conditions, understanding culture as the superstructure of society also brings a particular characteristic of these cohorts, which is their position concerning the post-capitalism world of the twenty-first century. (Gabriel, 2017)

A theoretical concept developed by Karl Marx[15], one of sociology's founders, refers to the production forces, or the materials and resources, which generate the goods society needs. Superstructure describes all other aspects of society. (Cole, 2020)

However, the German philosopher argued that it is not a 'neutral relationship' because a great deal depends on the

---

[15] Karl Heinrich Marx (1818-1883) was a German philosopher, critic of political economy, historian, sociologist, political theorist, journalist and socialist revolutionary. Born in Trier, Germany, Marx studied law and philosophy at the universities of Bonn and Berlin

superstructure -including culture, ideology, norms, and identities that people inhabit- 'emerges from the base' reflecting the ruling class's interests.

In the modern times of digitalization of a society of 'state capitalism' as Marx promoted and the high-speed internet advancing, we become more 'social entities.' (Ozollo, 2015, p 125)[16]

As the international magazine *The Economist* (2010) considered:

"Michael Wesch, who pioneered the use of new media in his cultural anthropology classes at Kansas State University, is also skeptical, saying that many of his incoming students have only a superficial familiarity with the digital tools that they use regularly, especially when it comes to the tools' social and political potential. Only a small fraction of students may count as true digital natives, in other words. The rest are no better or worse at using technology than the rest of the population.

Writing in The British Journal of Education Technology in 2008, a group of academics led by Sue Bennett of the University of Wollongong set out to debunk the whole idea of digital natives, arguing that there may be "as much variation within the digital native generation as between the generations". They caution that the idea of a new generation that learns in a different way might be counterproductive in education, because such sweeping generalizations "fail to

---

[16] We speak of **state capitalism** to refer to the phenomenon that occurs when, in an economic system with capitalist functioning, the State operates as an economic agent through companies that belong to it or that it manages directly or indirectly; this intervention of the State can be in certain sectors of the economy or cover the entire economic reality.

It may or may not work through state monopolies. In any case, it involves an intervention by an economic agent that is not on equal terms with others (if any) so it will affect free competition in a very negative way.

This phenomenon has occurred frequently throughout history; already in the Modern Age with mercantilism the State had a very important role in economic reality. However, in this article we are going to focus on the most current epoch in which there is a true capitalist system.

recognize cognitive differences in young people of different ages, and variation within age groups." The young do not really have different kinds of brains that require new approaches to school and work, in short." (Monitor)

As digital natives, most have a close relationship with technology, and their modes of consumption are far from the traditional methods of neoliberal capitalism. Moreover, 88% of Latin American digital natives have profiles on social networks. Their use does not respond only to peer-to-peer communication but is an integral part of their life in society.

The term describes a young person growing up in the digital age, in close contact with computers, the Internet and video game consoles, and later mobile phones, social networks, and tablets. (Prensky, 2001, p 3)

The term is often used to refer to Millennials, Generation Z and Generation Alpha[17]; the latter two are sometimes described as distinct "neo-digital natives" (Thomas, 2011, p 190 & Takahashi, 2016) from the "true" ones (Francis & Hoefel, 2018) or "digital integrators." (McCrindle & Fell, 2015, p 134)

They are distinguished from digital immigrants, who grew up before the advent of the Internet, reached the age of majority in a world dominated by print and television, and acquired familiarity with digital systems in adulthood. (Prensky, 2001, p 5)

These terms are often used to describe the digital generation gap regarding the technology's usability between people born after 1980 and those born before. (Zaphiris & Ioannou, 2018, p 34)

The terms of analogy between natives and immigrants, which refer to the relationships of age groups with the Internet and their

---

[17] Millennials, also known as Generation Y or Gen Y, are the demographic next generation X and previous generation Z. Researchers and popular media use the early 1980s as initial birth years and from the mid-1990s to the early 2000s as final birth years, with 1981 to 1996 being a widely accepted range of definition for the generation. Most millennials are children of baby boomers and early Gen Xers; Millennials are often the parents of Generation Alpha.

understanding, were used as early as 1995 by John Perry Barlow[18]. In an interview (Tunbridge, 1995) and used again in 1996 as part of his Declaration of Independence from *Cyberspace.* (Fededav, 2020)

The specific terms "digital native" and "digital immigrant" were popularized by education consultant Marc Prensky (2001) in his article entitled *Digital Natives, Digital Immigrants,* in which he relates the recent decline of American education to the inability of educators to understand the needs of learning on modern students. (Quảng Cáo, 2013)

His article postulated that "the advent and rapid diffusion of computer technology in the last decade of the twentieth century" had changed the way students think and process information, making it difficult for them to excel academically using the outdated teaching methods of the day.

In other words, children raised in a media-saturated digital world require a media-rich learning environment to maintain their attention, and Prensky (2001) called these children "digital natives."

It also goes on to say that digital natives have "spent their entire lives surrounded by and using computers and video games, digital music players, video cameras, cell phones, and all the other toys and tools of the digital age." (Prensy, 2001, p 3 & Gavin et al., 2013, p 550)

Marc Prensky (2001) defines digital natives as "native speakers" of the digital language of computers, videos, video games, social media, and other sites on the Web. Since then, Prensky (2009) has abandoned his native digital metaphor in favor of "digital wisdom."

"In 2001, I published "Digital Natives and Immigrants," a bipartite article that explained these terms to understand the

---

[18] John Perry Barlow (October 3, 1947 – February 7, 2018) was an American poet, essayist, cattle rancher, and political activist associated with both the Democratic and Republican parties. He was Fellow Emeritus at Harvard University's Berkman Klein Center for Internet & Society. (People, 2016)

profound differences between young people and numerous adults (Prensky 2001a, 2001b). While many have found these terms helpful, today, transiting the twenty-first century in which everyone will have grown up in the age of digital technology, the distinction between natives and immigrants will become less and less relevant.

As we work to create and improve the future, we need to imagine a new system of distinctions. I suggest we think in terms of digital wisdom.

"Digital technology can make us wiser and wiser. Digital wisdom is a double concept: it refers, first of all, to the wisdom that is presented in the use of technology, with which our cognitive capacity reaches beyond our natural capacity. And secondly, to wisdom in the prudent use of technology to enhance our capabilities. Thanks to technology we will have immediate access to all recorded history, libraries, all case studies and all data of any kind, and above all to highly realistic simulations that will facilitate our work." (Prensky, 2009)

More recently, the idea of the digital visitor and resident has been proposed as an alternative to understanding the several ways in which people relate to the existing technologies. It is also argued that digital natives and immigrants are labels that oversimplified the classification scheme. Some categories can be considered "indeterminate" from the framework of the previous assignments. (Sharpe, Beetham & Freitas, 2010, p 104)

Criticism of Prensky's conceptualization has resulted in further refinement of the terms. (Spear, 2007) For example, natives have been classified into three: those who *avoid,* minimalists, and *enthusiastic participants.* Evaders do not rely on technological devices and use technology even more, while minimalists use trends, although not as often as the active participants. (Zaphiris & Ioannou, 2018, p 100)

Because many digital immigrants are accustomed to a life without technology, they can sometimes disagree with the natives in their view. But, on the other hand, the daily regime of working life is becoming more technologically advanced with improved computers in offices, more complex machinery in the industry, and so on.

This can make it difficult for digital immigrants to keep pace, creating conflicts between older supervisors and managers and an increasingly younger workforce. (Quảng Cáo, 2013)

Similarly, parents bump into their kids at home over games, texting, YouTube, Facebook, and other internet technology issues. Much of the world's Gen Z and Millennials are digital natives. (Shapiro, 2012)

According to law professor and educator John Palfrey (Musgrove, 2008), there may be substantial differences between natives and non-digital natives regarding how people view relationships and institutions and access information. (Idem)

Despite this, the timetable for training young and old in recent technologies is the same. (Salajan, Schonwetter & Cleghorn, 2010, p 1398)

Prensky says education is the biggest problem facing the digital world. The immigrant instructors who speak an ancient language (that of the pre-digital age) struggle to teach a population that speaks an entirely new language.

Digital natives have had greater exposure to technology, which has changed how they interact and respond to devices. (Morgan, 2014, p 22) To meet the unique learning needs of the natives, teachers must move away from traditional teaching methods that are disconnected from the way students learn now. (Idem)

For the past decades, technical training for teachers has been at the forefront of policies. (Lei, 2009, p 89) However, immigrants suffer complications in teaching natives how to understand an environment that is "native" to them and alien to immigrants. Teachers struggle with proficiency levels and their skills to integrate technology into the classroom and show resistance towards integrating digital tools. (Hicks, 2011, p 190)

Since technology can be frustrating and complicated at times, some teachers worry about maintaining their level of professionalism within the classroom. Teachers worry about appearing "unprofessional" in front of their students. (p 191)

Although technology is challenged in the classroom, it is still essential for teachers to understand how natural and useful these digital tools are for students.

To meet the unique learning needs of the natives, Forzani and Leu (2012, p 422) suggest that electronic tools can immediately respond to today's students' natural, exploratory, and interactive learning styles.

Learning to use these digital tools provides unique learning opportunities for the natives and the necessary skills that will define their future success in the digital age. One preference for this problem is to invent computer games to teach them the lessons they need to learn, no matter how serious they are. (González-Munné, 2014, p 101)

This ideology has already been introduced in several practical severe aspects. For example, piloting a UAV[19] on the axis consists of someone sitting in front of a computer screen issuing commands to the UAV through a handheld controller that resembles, in detail, the model of controllers used to play games on an Xbox 360 game console. (p 115)

Gamification as a teaching tool has sparked interest in education, and Gee (2012) suggests this is because games have unique properties that books cannot offer to digital natives. (p 419)

For example, gamification provides an interactive environment for students to engage and practice twenty-first-century skills such as collaboration, critical thinking, problem-solving, and digital literacy.

---

[19] Unmanned aerial vehicle

Gee presents four reasons why gamification provides a distinct way of learning to promote twenty-first-century skills. First, games are based on problem-solving and not on one's ability to memorize the content. Second, gamification fosters creativity in the natives, where they are encouraged to think like a designer or modify to redesign games. Third, they are beginning to co-author their games through their decisions to solve problems and face challenges.

Therefore, students' thinking is stimulated to promote metacognition (Helsper & Enyon, 2009, p. 515) as they must think about their choices and how they will alter the course and outcome of the game. Finally, digital natives can collaborate and learn in a more social environment through online games.

Based on the literature, you can see digital tools' potential and valuable benefits. For example, online games help the natives meet their unique learning needs. In addition, online gaming seems to provide an interactive and engaging environment that promotes the necessary skills that they will need to succeed in their future.

Not everyone agrees with the language and underlying connotations of the native. (Holton et al., 2010 & Monitor, 2010) The term, by definition, suggests a familiarity with technology that not all children and young adults who would be considered the natives have; some, on the other hand, have discomfort with technology that not all digital immigrants have.

For example, those on the disadvantaged side of the digital divide lack access to technology. In its application, the concept of the natives prefers those who grow up with technology as possessing a special status, ignoring the significant difference between familiarity and creative application.

It is a particular way of understanding/interpreting reality through (or how it is perceived from and from) social media/the internet. Practically we mean abbreviations, common distortions of words, emoticons, emojis, memes, gifs. It already has armed dialogues, macro images, successions of phrases, and visual elements in its most advanced forms.

While the Internet was initially limited exclusively to written language—through applications such as email, chats, and word processors, they lacked higher levels of interaction -such as body language or tone in the voice. The gradual advancement of its use has been developing substitutes or adaptations of these lost levels.

You develop features that enable you to customize conversations and text -such as the ability to change the color and size- or demonstrate emotion by including punctuation to simulate images or expressions. Later, with emoticons, measures have been developed justly to compensate for the lack of face-to-face interaction.

To utterly understand the digital language, let us refer to the lecture of John McWhorter (2013) in his analysis of texting or texting—communication via text message by cell— at a *TED Talk* conference. He proposes to separate the new digital phenomenon from written language and instead compares it to the conversation. (McWhorter, 2013)

He explained how literature or written language a thoughtful and conscious activity is instead almost artistic, while the oral conversation is something much more primitive and inherent to the human being, whose main objective is functionality and in the new technological era has been translated into texting or, in our terms, digital language.

Moreover, the past linguists have identified that informal oral communication speaks in sentences of between seven and ten words, a model very much in line with how exchanges occur on digital platforms when the interactions that those platforms facilitate occur, as a digital service facilitating those exchanges.

The particularities of an electronic, written language serve a more subtle purpose than intonations, micro-expressions, or gestures used during a face-to-face conversation, mainly since today's generations live in a digital world, spending hours online. (Omar & Miah, 2013, p. 3)

Written language has adapted to the digital world with linguistic deformations, especially abbreviations. Other communicative elements such as photography and video seek their place in the interaction to achieve complete and complex communication, including new types. In a publication of OECD[20], Ramos and Schleicher (2018) expressed:

"Twenty-first century students live in an interconnected, diverse and rapidly changing world. Emerging economic, digital, cultural, demographic and environmental forces are shaping young people's lives around the planet and increasing their intercultural encounters on a daily basis. This complex environment presents an opportunity and a challenge. Young people today must not only learn to participate in a more interconnected world but also appreciate and benefit from cultural differences. Developing a global and intercultural outlook is a process – a lifelong process – that education can shape (Barrett et al., 2014; Boix Mansilla and Jackson, 2011; Deardorff, 2009; UNESCO, 2013, 2014a, 2016)" (p 4)

---

[20] The Organization for Economic Co-operation and Development is an intergovernmental economic organization with 38 member countries, founded in 1961 to stimulate economic progress and world trade.

Technological expertise is becoming increasingly important. Just as specialized tools are continuously developed, students must learn to use various recent technologies. In addition, most jobs will demand improved digital skills as we begin to integrate technological innovations into most professions.

Students must learn to be comfortable with existing technological tools, such as Internet search, word processing, spreadsheets, and social media applications, and that they feel comfortable learning innovative technologies. (Fadel, Bialik & Trilling, 2015, p 56)

The dilemma for teachers is that the most effortless skills to teach and assess are also the most specific skills to digitize, automate, and outsource. Undoubtedly, the most advanced knowledge in a discipline will always remain important.

Innovative or creative people usually have specialized skills in a field of knowledge or practice. And just as the skills to learn are essential, we always learn by learning something.

Educational success no longer reproduces content knowledge but instead extrapolates from what we know and applies that knowledge to new situations. The world no longer rewards people just for what they know – search engines know everything – but for what they can do from what they know, how they behave in the world, and how they adapt.

Cell phones, tablets, computers, wearables, among others, are some of the means used for digital communication. You cannot do without their qualities to identify how the media has fostered the forms of messages interaction within Marshall McLuhan's own rules. His popularized conclusion is that "the medium is the message,"[21] in his book *Understanding Media. The Extensions of Man.* (1964)

Thus, these means for their versatility and notably their low cost – economic, energy, and others– in transmitting information have privileged the image over the text. This technological privilege has been used to give way to a broader range of content, unlike previous technologies such as radio, television, or printing.

In terms of privacy, Professor Lori Kendall (2002) wrote that the anonymous and spontaneous nature of online chat rooms tends to blur the distinction between public and private in computer-mediated speech analysis (Kendall, 2002, p.60), something that we ought to be conscious.

Meanwhile, the issue of digital identity is complex, as it must consider the online footprint of any given entity, individual, or company, as well as the virtual and public nature of the medium and the tendency to reinvent one's identity through personal descriptions. (Zloteanu, 2018, p. 19)

---

[21] "In a culture like ours, long accustomed to splitting and dividing all things as a means of control, it is sometimes a bit of a shock to be reminded that, in operational and practical fact, the medium is the message. This is merely to say that the personal and social consequences of any medium—that is, of any extension of ourselves—result from the new scale that is introduced into our affairs by each extension of ourselves, or by any new technology. Thus, with automation, for example, the new patterns of human association tend to eliminate jobs it is true. That is the negative result. Positively, automation creates roles for people, which is to say depth of involvement in their work and human association that our preceding mechanical technology had destroyed." (McLuhan, 1964, p.23)

As Peck (2017) put it:

"Technologies provide users with structure while also leaving potential for individualization and variation inside that structure. It does, however, reflect a social pressure that can help us understand the emergence of expectations that undergird a practice. Hence, when discussing the changing nature of how vernacular practices circulate in the digital age, I am neither speaking in absolutes nor determinants. Instead, I am referring to capabilities enabled by digital network technologies and seeking to understand the various ways in which users have engaged that potential. Digital network technologies are increasingly commonplace in everyday life." (p 32)

Digital identity is treated in the scientific literature within the area of cyberculture. For example, several authors have linked it to data encryption, privacy, Internet security (Camenisch, 2009, p 34), and phishing (Kirda & Kruegel, 2006, p 7).

It should be said that there are also authors who have treated digital identity in the business context and have related it to corporate intranets and social Web applications in companies (Aced et al., 2009a; Bancal et al., 2009).

On the other hand, the academic literature reflects the interest in the characteristics of computer communication that print new patterns of development of digital identities (Campbell, 2005, p 128) and the online behaviors of children, adolescents, ethnic groups, or gender differences. (Giones Valls & Serrat i Brustenga, 2010, p 2)

However, the contributions on this topic do not focus on the set of digital and informational skills, revealed as fundamental in recent years, which are the object of this work.

In this sense, the relationship between these skills and social, cultural, and academic activities, increasingly varied in the network, constitute a new topic of study that has not yet been sufficiently addressed in the scientific literature, as well as the construction of identity in the network in non-anonymous environments (Zhao et al., 2008, p 1830).

Some works that have dealt with digital identity from the perspective of multiliteracy are those of Perkel (2006) and Livingstone (2004, p 460).

In an intensely computerized society, one of the dangers is the difference between those who have access to modern technologies and those who do not. The gulf between those who know how to use them and those who do not. (Compaine, 2001

The latter becomes the new sector at risk of social exclusion, the digital divide phenomenon. Therefore, citizens must develop informational and digital skills to avoid this fracture's marginalization.

We can differentiate between the most basic skills, such as knowing how to read or manage a digital document, and the most advanced skills, such as coordinating a work team that cannot meet in person or doing procedures through electronic administration.

Among the new skills that the twenty-first-century citizen must acquire is the competence to manage the digital identity effectively. How do you build that?

Actively, it is done by contributing texts, images, and videos to the Internet, participating, in short, in the Web world. It is built from a user profile on social networking sites, which is often linked to profiles of other users or contacts.

A well-managed and homogeneous digital identity with analog identity impacts a more active life in all areas. Moreover, it consolidates a more solid social fabric outside the Internet. (Giones Valls & Serrat i Brustenga, 2010, p 3)

However, digital identity construction is inescapably linked to technological and informational skills and an energetic attitude in the network, participatory, open, and collaborative.

It can be configured in many ways, and the same person can

have different identities using different tools or have only one. From Gamero (2009), a series of free and accessible tools are presented on the network, through which anyone can structure it.

FACEBOOK, INSTAGRAM, AND OTHERS: FEEDING THE MONSTER

Social media, in general, have more than three billion users. Facebook alone, ads have a million daily, who spend an average of 35 minutes daily on the system. In general, the average daily time spent by users on social media is 116, accessing it 91% of them via mobile devices, contributing Facebook, Twitter, and LinkedIn contributed to 90% of social traffic. Users grew by 320 million between September 2017 and October 2018. (Srivastava, 2019)

Pohl et al. (2017) consider that:

"For more and more users, the mobile phone is their primary, or even only, computing device. On Facebook, e.g., mobile-only users make up a growing percentage of users, currently already accounting for more than 50 % of their monthly active users [Protalinski, 2016]. Facebook is but one of many messaging and social networking applications, that, overall, dominate the rankings for most used applications on mobile devices [Church et al. 2015]. As such, a critical aspect of mobile systems is how they can support the expression and creativity of their users, enabling them to connect with those dear to them. Text input is a dominant aspect of this expression and has hence been a research focus for many years. For example, researchers have designed many input methods to optimize text entry speeds (for a comparison see, e.g., [Kristensson & Vertanen, 2014]). But text input is not necessarily restricted to actual text. Instead of using characters to compose words, they can also be repurposed in emoticons, such as :), or r <3. Here, characters are put together in a way that disposes of their actual meaning and makes use of their look to assemble larger shapes. Hence, the colon turns into a set of eyes and the parenthesis becomes a mouth." (p 7)

Lately, it seems that social networks are our mirror because we show how we are or how we want to see ourselves in the eyes of others. It is certain that social networks feed our ego to such a degree of overflowing it. (Psico.mx)

Twitter, Facebook, Instagram, among other social networks, were created to facilitate communication with other people, meet others, and make us known. However, most of them are more inclined to "make us known."

Suppose you start to observe your profile and that of other people. In that case, most have content and images, even manipulated with Photoshop application and others, making it seem that the person looks perfect because they are portrayed with their best pose.

By saying that several people manipulate their photographs, we not only refer to give a retouching with countless applications to change filters or exposure to photography, but people through their social networks also work their photographs to show off or appear to the world how ideal their life is. So, others praise their tastes, your photos, etc.

In short, social networks increase your EGO, and it is exposed to others.

If we analyze a little more deeply, have you noticed that even you use them under the concept "I"? I look good on my profile. I take a photograph in which I look good and make me gain more popularity, I upload only those images where I look good, others do not matter; likewise, I show in my social networks that my family is perfect and united, I share only my tastes (only those that make me look good), and so on, social networks are always used under me, me, my; we focus excessively on looking good

Have you ever wondered why they do it or do we do it? We

find answers from the superficial, numbers to get more "likes," conquer someone, etc. Still, the reality is different. Your EGO is spreading through your social networks because you always want to be the center of everything, that everyone revolves around us.

The human being is vain by nature, we all are in different percentages, but there it is. In addition, it does not hurt that from time to time, we feed our Ego, as long as it is in a controlled way; however, social networks make us vulnerable, and that is when we fall into the need to exploit the Ego.

Vanity has always been present in them, and therefore they have it very well-identified. Consequently, it is expected that this feature is observed on Twitter, Facebook, Instagram, etc.

As Carmen Fishwick (2016) published in *The Guardian*

"Is social media turning a relatively modest species into a pack of publicity-hungry narcissists? Or were we already inherently self-absorbed?

In the US, diagnoses of narcissistic personality disorder (NPD) have risen sharply over the past 10 years: the rate of increase is comparable to the rise in the rate of obesity.

Numerous studies claim to have made direct links between the increase in NPD and the ubiquity of social media. Behaviors such as attempting to attract more followers, wanting to tell followers about your life, and the need to project a positive image always have been described by researchers as examples of exhibiting narcissistic personality traits on social media. A direct link has also been found between the number of Facebook friends a person has and the prevalence of socially disruptive characteristics commonly associated with narcissism."

EMOTICONS: CONVEYING OUR EMOTIONS

The emoticons emerged as combinations of text characters combined to represent gestures of the human face visually. A digital conversation, said, through a chat, allowed to express more information beyond the words, because with symbolism shared by receiver and sender, these new elements proposed by users in their social exchanges.

They have also fulfilled the function of compensating for the subtleties of natural nonverbal language in transmitting emotions. These symbols were adapted to acquire increasingly human characteristics, passing only from strokes of written language to cartoon-style representations of faces until finally adopting consistent qualities such as skin tone or hair color.

There is a fascinating case not only because of the significant growth and dominance in the social sphere of the Social Network *Facebook* but also because of the implications for global communication under the same symbols: the implementation of reactions in 2016, being used three hundred billion times since launch. (Hutchinson, 2017)

Throughout its brief history, this platform has gone into a gradual process towards humanization. From the implementation of emojis, stickers to the integration of native GIFs. In 2016, it provided users with a new way to interact with the contents by moving from the simple and iconic 'like' button to reactions.

The latter represents a technological and graphic evolution and social ones based on representations that could be said universally. Expressing basic human emotions, like anger, fear, disgust, happiness, sadness, and surprise (Mauss & Robinson, 2009, p. 10) hence, their use provides dynamic information to the related content. (Hauthal et al., 2019, p. 1)

The development and dissemination of digital technologies have profoundly changed our society. We have moved from an organizational and productive industrial model to *an information society*. One of the areas in which this technical revolution is most noticeable is the increasing use of these technological tools as an instrument for socialization and interpersonal communication.

As Dr. Hiranya K. Nath from the *Sam Houston State University* of Texas wrote in his article *The information society* (2009), paraphrasing Dr. Marc Uri Porat and Michael Rogers Rubin in their 1977 report sponsored by the *National Science Foundation:*

"In the information society where technology is the defining characteristic, information is defined in terms of the probabilities of occurrence of symbols and its quantity is measured in bits. In the economic exposition of the information society, information is defined as the "data that have been organized and communicated" (Porat and Rubin, 1977, p 22) (Nath, 2009, p 3)

The use of emoticons over time has evolved, their number has grown, and they have diversified, both in form and in function and intention. At first, they represented fundamental emotions. However, today, they form a complex and sometimes ambiguous group whose interpretation is increasingly difficult to perform since they seem to be highly dependent on the context in many cases. (Vandergriff, 2013, p 8)

However, they all have a communicative character that has led to creating a code between sender and receiver (Moral & García, 2003, p 134). Scientific research on emoticons on the Net began in the early nineties of the twentieth century.

Authors such as Lea and Spears (1992, p 323), Markus (1994, p 123), and Herring (1996, p 134) hypothesized that emoticons were special tools that could be used to compensate for the absence of emotional and social cues in online conversations.

These works often specified, in the words of Lea and Spears (1992, p. 321), that in computer-mediated communication, "the meaning of paralinguistic marks depends on
the individual or group context that is pre-established for communication." (Baron, 2009, p 115)

Other authors such as Kavanaugh, Carroll, Rosson, Zin, and Reese (2005, p 30), through different studies, concluded that paralinguistic signals in computer-mediated communication seemed to be more necessary in cases where people communicated with strangers rather than with acquaintances or friends.

In this line, Darics (2010, p 134) pointed out that the emoticon "smiley face" seems to be essential in work contexts to create a collaborative environment. Joe Walther and Kyle D'Addario in 2001 (p 325) studied the extent to which Internet users relied on the meaning of emoticons when interpreting the messages they received.

Their results pointed to the one-on-one online communication being interpreted by cyber speakers based more on verbal content than on emoticons. In addition, Postmes, Spears, and Lea (2000, p 352) concluded that the use of emoticons is highly variable from one online communication group to another. More importantly, the same user varies their use depending on their use on the participating one.

Byron and Baldridge (2007, p 132) found that personality was also a determining factor in the degree to which nonverbal cues were incorporated into online communication. (Cuadrado Gordillo, Martín-Mora Parra & Fernández Antelo, 2015, p 186)

ANTI-LANGUAGE EXPRESSIONS? "CYBER-SPELLING"

Misspellings on social media are often attributed to the writer's lack of concentration or awareness from the communicative proximity. Aware that the recipient of his message – usually a friend – is at both the conventions that govern communication on social media, the linguistic quality mainly refers to the degree of excellence of words in a text. (Baeza-Yates & Rello, 2011, p. 2)

However, in reality, these 'netizens' make use of a different spelling from that of standard texts, of an "anti-spelling," which does not prevent the utterance and its enunciator from being understood, since they share the same linguistic competencies (Zheng, 2018, p. 803). In this sense, academics used' anomie,' as the absence of norm." (Xiaoping, 2008, p. 223)

The former results from ignorance of the rules governing spelling, while the latter constitute what we might call intentional deviations. The latter group seems to respond to the duplication of vowels and consonants found in many messages. The issue of linguistic annotation with morphological *taggers* and parsers should be considered to fine-tune linguistic analysis. (Gries & Berez, 2017, p. 383)

Gretchen McCulloch (2019) considers that the internet and 'smart' mobile devices "have brought us an explosion of writing by normal people" (p 38). Of course, we write
information about anything when our texts and chats and posts more make formal writing disappear, never premeditated, unfiltered and mundane. (p 39)

Arafah, Hasyim, and Kapoyos (2021) expand that Netizens are a combination of the word's internet and citizens, meaning the citizens of the internet and the term 'parrhesia.'

"Digital democracy is an activity that uses social media as a form of netizens' participation in delivering facts and thoughts, both in the form of criticism or even support (Jha & Kodila-Tedika, 2020, p 282). In their capacity as scientists, professors, workers, civilians, and the general public, netizens have the courage to speak the truth or say the actual things without hiding anything. Foucault (2018, p 128) gave the term parrhesia which means to tell the truth or say what it is, and people who use parrhesia are called parrhesiasites. Parrhesia contains a moral obligation for someone to convey a truth for the public interest (Schmidt, 2011, p 48)." (p 423)

Parrhesia means "to say everything." To say everything, first, bravely say everything one has to say to anyone without being silent, speaking frankly and without fear.

From there, the term parrhesia takes on a second meaning, as harmful, in saying everything. It cannot shut up or keep anything because the importance of the distinction between what is thought and what can be said has been lost.

The *parrhesiastés*, adjective corresponding to the noun parrhesia, is the charlatan, the impertinent, or the dissipated.

And parrhesia still has a third meaning: that of the trust and openness that denotes or with which it occurs to be communicating frankly with another, without hiding anything from him and without looking to hide anything from him.

Parrhesia means security and trust in dealing with another, not fear in dealing with him. Foucault devoted his 1984 course at the College de France to the notion of parrhesia. It was Foucault's last course. It has been published under the title *Le courage de la verité*, and there are also recordings.

In this course, Foucault manages to collect in order and articulately these three meanings of parrhesia.

This means that this Foucault course in this aspect perhaps

also depends on the dictionary. Language is an outside administered in this case by the one who assists the lexicographic discourse, thus establishing a normative partage from which the scholar can be governed. (Jiméndez Redondo, 2012, p 121)

Going back to the concept of 'anti-language, Yusuf Bhana (2016) clarifies:

"Examples of anti-language can also be found online. While most anti-language is designed to be inaccessible, there are some current examples on the internet. There are, for example, a variety of words for sex work that indicate cryptolects are being used to communicate in full view of the world in a way that only a few can understand. Humans have such capacity for language that new ones are spontaneously created whenever circumstances demand one, and the internet is likely to have the effect of enabling closed groups to communicate with one another in a secret manner."

Some examples are Polari - used by the gay community, particularly around London, in the first two-thirds of the XXth century-; Cockney-rhyming slang -a collection of phrases used by some Londoners-; Grypsera -originally a polish dialect, borrows from Yiddish, Ukrainian, Russian, and German and is used as a criminal code by inmates of the Polish prison system. -; English pig Latin -gobbledygook anti-language takes a bit of getting used. In every case, the first consonant from a word is removed and replaced at the end of the term, followed by the addition of 'ay'' for example, the word 'language' becomes 'anguagelay'-; Jeringoso - the Spanish equivalent to Pig Latin-; Verlan -French anti-language. (Bhana, 2016)

FROM CONSUMERS TO PROSUMERS

The term "prosumer"[22] is still a sparsely widespread concept. Even though it emerged in the seventies of the last centuries, it is now in the 21st, when it is often used. The term is used to point to those users of the Network who assume the role of a communication channel, coined by Alvin Toffler in 1980 (Toffler, 1980, p. 12).

It has its origins in the union of two concepts: producer and consumer. Initially, it did not refer to the field of technology. Instead, it pointed to that individual who was doing activities for himself was linked to the economy: the producer who produces his products and consumes them, without intermediaries.

In the face of technological gaps, gaps in participation, and the use of technologies as a "power tool," arises the prosumer, who knows how means and mediation are carried out, which requires the place to be won to exercise a citizenry to the face of injustices. Only policies that implement valid and effective media and digital literacy will achieve citizen empowerment in the digital age.

In the digital sense, to be a prosumer is to be a citizen in the 2.0 environment, capable of producing and consuming information. It uses the growing set of multimedia tools that allow it to express itself and share with the citizens of cyberspace.

The postulates of the first thinkers who created and studied the term prosumer are still dormant today and can be analyzed-two and used for new digital media.

Social media is perhaps the means of providing the most immediate view of the prosumer. Everyone can be both a producer

---

[22] During the First Wave most people consumed what they themselves produced. They were neither producers nor consumers in the usual sense. They were instead what might be called "prosumers." (Toffler, 1980, p 266)

and distributor of communications. Another matter is whether this information is, in effect, relevant or not. But the user has in his hands this power even if he is not aware of it.

For most children and young people, the three most important screens are mobile phones, computers, and tv. Therefore, media education that contributes to an appropriate relationship with digital media can be producers and consumers is paramount.

The customer is now a participant in the production process, a prosumer. That is why Web 3.0 is taking on a real revolution for advertising, never known. As a result, this website can strengthen by being a tool of interaction, collaboration, or even learning and by being a powerful marketing tool. (Sánchez-Carrero & Contreras - Pulido, 2012, p 72)

We live in a time characterized by an almost inexhaustible digital revolution due to the speed of its changes and the roles that citizens are adopting. As a result, institutions, social groups, and individuals face dynamics in which their action takes center stage, giving them a higher possibility of decision and empowering them hugely.

The implementation of media education requires a determined and natural impulse. This will contribute to a prosumer individual with many more potentialities.

Training to produce and consume information in a conscious, ethical, and effective way will be a step forward in developing the citizen committed to himself and his environment.

In *Fearless Speech*, Michael Focault (2001) presents this brilliant concept:

"My intention was not to deal with the problem of truth, but with the problem of the truth-teller, or of truth-telling as an activity: ... who is able to tell the truth, about what, with what consequences, and with what relations to power .... [W]ith the question of the importance of telling the truth, knowing who is able to tell the truth, and knowing why we should tell the truth, we have the roots of what we could call the; critical' tradition in the West." (p 5)

Currently, most of the world's citizens are aware of the problems in society and the environment, and we want to be part of their solution. We citizens want to act to benefit those who live in poverty, marginalization, and exclusion. Still, we are also aware that factors in our behavior affect society, for example, the environment. (Worldcoo, 2014)

"Prosumers" are those consumers who become content producers of a product or service. They provide information or opinions about a product or service in different applications or websites. They produce content about their experience with the product or service.

In the imaginary of the ubiquity society, digital communications have a definite impact on the development and evolution of new communicative environments. Today, the "sender" and "receiver" systems and the models that yesterday allowed the communicative process to be explained exhibit apparent limitations in their explanatory capacities. (Islas, 2008, p 69)

Reality has overwhelmed them. In the historical development of the media, it is possible to notice how they resent specific remedies. From the perspective of media ecology, the Internet – the intelligent means of messages transmission – admits to being understood as a logical extension of the telegraph.

The telegraph represented the first externalization of our nervous system. The development of mobile digital messaging moves us toward a new media environment: the
society of ubiquity. According to Neil Postman (1986), behind all technology lies a philosophy and the communicative principles of it: communication for all, at anytime, anywhere, displace with them the need to produce the ideal mobile digital devices to respond to the demands of the communicative environment that this society supposes. (Islas-Carmona, 2008, p 29)

The development of Web 2.0 admits to being considered as a

truly historical watershed in the evolution of the Internet; this imposed essential changes in both the behavior and cultural consumption habits of netizens. Therefore, the netizen agreed to the condition of the prosumer.

We must recognize prosumers as the communicative actors of the society of ubiquity. The role of prosumers will be definitive in the following remediations that the Internet will experience, a medium that definitively admits to being understood as a logical extension of human intelligence.

However, before that, in precisely 1972, Marshall McLuhan and Barrington Nevitt had worked together on a book titled *Take Today: The Executive as Dropout* (1972), in which they referred to technological environments and how they would influence the role of the man as producer and consumer, the prosumer.

Visionary professor Marshal McLuhan raised his hypotheses two decades in advance, noticing what would happen in society, signing that all media are extensions of some faculty of the human being. Whether mental or physical and that the content of a medium is, justly another means:

"This fact, characteristic of all media, means that the "content" of any medium is always another medium. The content of writing is speech, just as the written word is the content of print, and print is the content of the telegraph." (McLuhan, 1964, p. 10)

He goes around each media and devotes an in-the-house section to technological determinism, explaining what it would mean to live in an automated world, as he perceived the future, with the effects of technology. (Adler, 2008, p. 1538-1539). He does so by recalling the history of the man:

"It is not an exaggeration to say that the future of modern society and the stability of its inner life depend in large part on the maintenance of an equilibrium between the strength of the techniques of communication and the capacity of the individual's own reaction." (McLuhan, 1964, p. 28)

As Dr. Mario Carlón from the University of Buenos Aires, Argentina (FCPolitUNR, 2011) stated, in a conference, it is not about recovering McLuhan to think about the problems of mediation in our day. It is about regaining their thinking based on the effect of the "rearview mirror"[23] – which asserted that civilizations, therefore societies and generations, always look at those that have preceded them (the past), while living in the present. (Czitrom, 1982, p 156)

It is necessary to retake the knowledge produced by McLuhan about the media. It gives a very graphic example: the television live occurs just like the mirror. But, conversely, other media such as Skype complicate these processes.

Carlon, during his lecture at McLuhan's Hundred Years Conference 1911-2011:

"Skype returns in shorts below an image, which is like an image in the mirror, which you are talking about. (...) A kind of complex construction of the cascading subject, which in turn brings particular problems by the way this is organized. (...) In Skype the image appears inverted. Thus, a particular construction of the subject occurs because the camera is not like the mirror. It is similar but not the same. (FCPolitUNR, 2011)

Indeed, talking on *Skype* can become a standardized action performed without any preparation. Again, not knowing the system but understanding what a live stream is, what the Internet means, what an interface is, and others—in this case, strengthening relationships with the combination of a video and voice call.

Faced with this dynamism of problems, there has been a promiscuous and polymorphous invocation of the concept of ethical responsibility. Scientists should conduct their research responsibly.

---

[23] Refers to *The Global Village* (1996) (McLuhan, 1964). *Understanding media. The extensions of man*. New York, NY: Signet Books.

Doctors must have a responsibility to their patients. Engineers ensure public safety, health, and welfare when designing structures, products, processes, and systems. Entrepreneurs have a responsibility to commercialize science and technology for public benefit.

The population is recommended to practice responsible sexuality. Consumers need to be responsible users of the devices and opportunities that saturate the world of technological life. Governments must be accountable to their citizens, companies to their investors, schools to their students.

In so many contexts, what is responsibility? The call for commitment permeates the entire traditional ethical discourse, whether it is focused on virtue, rights, contracts, utility, or duty.

While responsibility is present in accepted moral theory, it is yet to be revealed or interpreted. In fact, in English, the abstract name "responsibility" (though not the adjective "responsible") is only a few hundred years old. Nevertheless, it has acquired cultural and ethical importance in the legal, religious, engineering, scientific, and philosophical contexts precisely within its progressive interactions with technology. Thus, one way to reflect on the meaning of responsibility begins with reviewing this story.

Initiatives to address these new dimensions of responsibility lie in philosophy and popular culture, in the form of comic book superheroes. Spider-Man is an especially poignant example.

After being bitten by a radioactive spider in a scientific laboratory, Peter Parker becomes possessed of great powers that carry extraordinary responsibilities. As Parker later reflects, the result is that "the choice of leading a normal life is no longer an option." That is the weight of responsibility in the presence of technological powers. (Mitcham, 2012, p 173 & Pauli, 2008)

More than 20 years have passed since the birth of the world computer network, better known as the World Wide Web (1989), and more than 40 years after creating the Internet (1969). Indeed, to some extent, it has left its mark whatever the date of our debut as internet users, especially since one of the most attractive fields of the Network since 2003 has been the user's participation in Web 2.0 tools, whose main feature is the sharing of information.

The task of interacting and being part of the collaborative work has altered the primal idea that the Internet existed solely for information, as Web 1.0 was known. Creating content and allowing others to know them, use them, and transform them, has also provided the user with a generous feeling of contributing without expecting anything in return that is not some comment indicating that it has been helpful to the published information.

Of course, there are also negative experiences resulting from the misuse of a website. For example, sexting - pornographic content via mobile - and cyberbullying for minors are sufficient. As the *Handbook of Communication and Social Skills* called: "The history of the discipline of communication (broadly conceived) is the story of identifying, investigating and teaching social skills." (Wiemann, 2003. p. ix)

The truth is that blogs, wikis, audiovisual channels such as *YouTube* and *Vimeo*, photo portals such as *Flickr*, dedicated to music such as Last.fm, educational platforms such as virtual classrooms or campuses, and social networks make up a large part of that universe of the user participation as a producer and consumer. It involves a different approach to market-sharing, giving, and receiving.

In a report of the *PEW Research Center*, Janna Anderson and

Lee Rainie (2018) collected opinions about *The Negatives of digital Life*: These one-liners from anonymous respondents hit on several different themes:

- "Digital technologies have made it more difficult for me to say on task and devote sustained attention. This interferes with my work productivity."
- "I can't seem to get my brain to calm down and focus. It is all over the place. I can't concentrate. I just start thinking about what I'm going to do next."
- "Increased isolation is a negative effect I feel in my life; the time I spend using digital technologies could well be spent in other more creative and productive ways."
- "I am becoming increasingly aware of the way constant access to digital forms of communication can be overwhelming."
- "It has become an ever-present overhang on all aspects of life. There is no escape."
- "The rise of hatred, the manipulation of politics and so on – these are not distant events with no personal impact."
- "Digital life has tipped the balance in favor of John Stuart Mill's 'lower pleasures' and has made engaging in higher-order pleasures more difficult."
- "One major impact is the overall decrease in short-term memory, and … what was the question?"
- "Real-life relationships are less bearable; everyone is so much less interesting with the spoiling of technology."
- "Digital technology radically increases expectations for instantaneous responses. This is unhealthy."
- "It has become harder to take your eyes off a screen to enjoy life as it's happening."
- "Technology is being driven by business across all areas for money, money, money. Greed has taken over."
- "Engagement with technology is starting very young, and

we don't really know what the impact will be."
- "We don't understand what we can trust anymore."

The digital world and its communication present a particular logic. When written through the networks, anonymity and impunity facilitate the emergence of aggressive and offensive speech, the so-called hate speeches.

The European Commission defines hate speech *against Racism and Intolerance* as the encouragement, promotion, or instigation of hatred, humiliation, or contempt of a person or group of persons in any of its forms. Also, like harassment, discredit, dissemination of negative stereotypes, stigmatization or threat concerning that person or group of people and the justification of such manifestations on the grounds of 'race,' color, ancestry, national or ethnic origin, age, disability, language, religion or belief, sex, gender, gender identity, sexual orientation, and other personal characteristics or conditions. (ECRI, 2014, p 32, 37)

Hate speech on the internet has its characteristics. In this way, they differ from hate speech that is transmitted verbally. In the networks, the capacity of diffusion and transmission of these discourses expands exponentially, generating the so-called phenomenon of 'viralization,' which describes the massive way in which digital messages expand over the Internet in a brief period.

In addition, another of the main characteristics of hate speech is the durability of these messages. Those are absorbed and 'immortalized' by the networks themselves, captured and reused repeatedly. (Bustos Martínez, 2019)

The revolution of information and communication technologies -mainly due to the expansion of the Internet and its tools throughout the globe-presents a new communicative paradigm, where social relations and information exchanges will hardly return to the way they were before.

In this way, the information society generates a social

structure based on the massive exchange of knowledge, which is transmitted through the communication networks of the new digital technologies, creating a global information society in constant interaction. (Soler, 2020)

This paradigm generates a new context full of opportunities and challenges. That is, of positive and negative possibilities. The Internet is not liberating or democratizing in itself. Still, it can produce "different political results in different environments" and, therefore, it is advisable not to be carried away by 'technological solutionism' or *cyberutopism.* (Morozov 2012)

Citizen responsibility plays a fundamental role because it will be possible to end hate speeches and crimes through the education and dissemination of this problem. Thanks to awareness and social awareness, citizens will be better able to identify and stop hate speech on networks, and, therefore, they can be neutralized more effectively.

It is a challenge that encompasses the whole of society as a whole; institutions, citizens a day, must tackle online hate speech through instruction, training, individual will, and civic behavior (Hassan, 2019).

Social networks make the professional a much more active user who takes advantage of the means to generate opinions or recommend endless activities.

One of the most prominent examples is *Twitter* by US President Barack Obama (@barackobama). A high-level representative who once would have had no contact with citizens beyond mere political encounters - with some distance - is now coming close via Twitter.

He or his team – writes phrases daily, uploads videos, and recommends links that express his thinking, especially during the election campaign season.

One classic provocateur, ex-president Donald Trump, go to the extreme in the use of incendiary language, as Dr. Oscar Winberg commented in the *European Journal of American Studies* (2017, p 6):

"Despite the long tradition of both insult politics and right-wing populism in the United States, the mocking rhetoric used by Donald Trump in the presidential campaign was widely perceived and described as norm-breaking and extreme.[24] For example, the New York Times editorial board explicitly cited the Republican nominee's insults in an editorial titled "Why Donald Trump Should Not Be President." The editorial listed the qualities of the New York businessperson as "bluster, savage mockery of those who challenge him, degrading comments about women, mendacity, crude

---

[24] See, for example, Jose A. DelReal, "Trump Draws Scornful Rebuke for Mocking Reporter with Disability," *Washington Post* (2015); Holly Yan, "Donald Trump's 'Blood' Comment about Megyn Kelly Draws Outrage," *CNN.com* (2015), and Ben Schreckinger, "Trump Attacks McCain: 'I Like People Who Weren't Captured,'" *Politico* (2015).

generalizations about nations and religions."[25]

In recent years, five have been the events that have transformed the social and technological life of consumers. The first of these was the emergence of the Internet on November 21, 1969, creating the first link between UCLA and Stanford universities through the switched telephone line.

The second was the first personal computer's appearance with the Olivetti Programma 101 (1965) and the Apple II (1977). The third was the appearance of the IBM Simon Personal Communicator on November 23, 1992, con-
the first smartphone. Finally, the fourth event was the appearance of the first social network, classmates, in 1995 that allowed its users to contact former classmates. (Sarmiento Guede, Curiel & Antonovica, 2017)

The latest and no less important event has been the evolution that has led from Web 1.0, created in 1990 by the Englishman Tim Berners-Lee with the help of the Belgian Robert Cailliau to Web 2.0, a term first term used by Tim O'Reilly in 2004. These events have changed the way consumers interact with organizations by going from an analog context to a digital context and modifying their attitudes and behaviors towards the brand message. (Sarmiento et al., 2017, p 71)

Consumers have replaced traditional media (Hann et al., 2008 cited in Hinz et al., 2011) with social media. Numerous research papers and justifying our development show that social media are the most important interfaces to spread the product message. Still, all this depends mainly on the voluntary participation of users. At this point, viral marketing emerges as a process in which the trade message can connect with users (Paus & Macchia, 2014).

In January 2016, around 3,419 million people used the Internet, and 2,307 million had a presence on some social media

---

[25] Editorial Board, *Why Donald Trump Should Not Be President, New York Times.* (2016)

(World Population Statistics, 2016 & (Sarmiento Guede, Curiel & Antonovica, 2017). The data reflects the importance of the Internet as a Marketing and Communication channel.

Most of these users participate in social media (Albors et al., 2008, p 198). Electronic word of mouth has become a new form of communication (Gremler et al., 2003, p 41). In general, social media provides new opportunities for users to share their opinions about products or services (Chen & Xie, 2008, p 484; Adams et al., 1999, p 45) and make them the new brand influencers.

Kaplan and Haenlein (2010, p 61) define social media as "a group of Internet-based applications that are based on the ideological and technological foundations of Web 2.0, which enables the creation and sharing of user-generated content."

Recently, Buettner (2016) has defined social media as "computer-mediated technologies that enable users, businesses, NGOs, governments, and other organizations to visualize, create and share information, ideas, professional interests and other forms of expression across virtual communities and networks."

There are numerous definitions of the term, but most have some characteristics in common, such as the following (Obar & Wildman, 2015).

The first transmission models were unidirectional, one-to-many, in which the brand transmitted information through a medium (press, television, radio, etc.) to consumers. This model of mass communication tried to emulate the traditional model of the process, but it lacked the essential element to be able to develop it: interaction.

According to Schultz and Peltier (2013, p 15), communication does not exist without interaction. With the advent of the Internet and, in particular, social media, the traditional model was simplified into a more personalized one.

Over the last few years, the user has undergone a great

transformation. It has ceased to be a passive actor in becoming an active actor. As a result, he controls excellent information and has a great power of influence over others through his opinions.

Word of mouth communication, the Internet, and social media have developed a new phenomenon called viral marketing as a new technique to generate positive or negative interaction about brands. (Sarmiento Guede, Curiel & Antonovica, 2017)

DIGITAL ILLITERACY

Write on a blog, record a video, edit it, take photos, make a virtual photo album, draw a bullet, record a podcast, design a presentation in *PowerPoint, Prezi,* or others. All of these are possible actions for an active internet user who takes advantage of the benefits of the Network by uploading content, exchanging ideas, sharing, negotiating, and others. However, not all users have the same activities, but it depends heavily on their reality.

Nevertheless, perhaps more important than age, another factor is the zero or poor preparation in the school and family system to train as producers and consumers. Therefore, they are more consumers than producers on the Network. The veil covers the actual illiteracy in which many are immersed that they are digital natives.

However, they were born in the age of technological convergence and have access - not all, must point it out - to the digital medium are experts and properly unfolding as prosumers? No, absolutely.

There are barriers to access unfathomable technologies in multiplatform interaction projects for social dialogue and its praxis – in the Freireani (Freire, 2005) sense of reflection and action – outside the cultural industry.

Transmedia narratives presuppose digital connection and convergence and assume, on the one hand, the stable provision of the internet, and on the other, full social participation, dismissing digital illiteracy.

Digital illiteracy is different from the inability to read and write and understand messages, "although many people can read and/or write without major difficulties, it turns out that these skills are insufficient to access the communication/information network that emanates from new technologies" (Rosas, 2012). For this reason, the digitally illiterate carry out all their activities outside the use of information and communication technologies (ICT). Still, they would not reach a full insertion in the digital era of the XXI century by the same time. (Yépez-Reyes, 2018, p 285)

Digital literacy entails unexpected challenges and encounters with new mental paradigms typical of the digital age. These new paradigms have had some responsibility in the so-called "digital divide," which has opened since the beginning of globalization, dissociating those who have access to ICTs[26] and those who do not. Haight et al. (2014, p 515) argue that the digital divide must be analyzed from three fronts: internet access, online activity level, and social networks.

It should be noted that this digital divide does not only occur between affluent and impoverished countries but also between regions within the same country, between social groups and generations, and not exclusively in developing countries.

Terms such as "computer literacy, computational literacy, ICT literacy, e-literacy, network literacy, media literacy and others that circumvent the idea of 'literacy' such as a computer or informational fluency." (Bawden, 2008 p. 17)

That preceded the establishment of the term "digital literacy" as we understand it today.

The term "digital literacy" was coined by Paul Gilster (1997) in his seminal work Digital Literacy (Gutiérrez Martín, 2003; Meyers, Erickson, & Small, 2013), referring to the ability to understand and use information through computers. The author is energetic in clarifying that "it is not simply a question of reading, but of understanding, of thinking critically" (Gilster, 1997, p. 3, quoted by Gutiérrez, 2003).

Meyers, Erickson, and Small (2013) analyze how digital literacy has been studied across different disciplines, without

---

[26] Technologies of information and communication.

privileging technology over the acquisition of knowledge, and classify the study of digital literacy into three distinct approaches: 1) acquisition of digital skills, 2) digital cognitive models and 3) involvement in digital cultures and practices.

The first approach aims to acquire skills typical of the digital age, which despite being contemporary technologies, are based on the generation of adaptations of the knowledge previously gained outside the digital. In this way, a digitally literate individual can effectively employ digital resources to solve information, knowledge, or understanding needs.

The second perspective emphasizes adopting abstract cognitive models to understand activities with digital content. These models underpin problem-solving capabilities and the construction of mental structures of thinking and evaluating media messages.

The third perspective, instead, looks at digital literacy as a group of emerging practices involving individual capacities that are socially constructed and that serve in general for life, for learning, and for work in a society, which recognizes the changing nature of technology and is aware of the future expectations of citizens.

It is essential to bring up the multidimensional proposal that Lankshear and Knobel (2008) make for using the plural "digital literacies" to illustrate this term's multiple facets. The authors consider that it would be reductionist to concentrate all of them in the singular within a single literacy.

On the other hand, Livingstone et al. (2011) point out, among the myths that children have on the Internet, the following: "Digital natives know everything" and "Everyone is creating their content." Concerning the former, the idea that children know more than their parents are exaggerated.

Mobile digital communications lead us to a society where we can be everywhere at the time. But, on the other hand, so far, young people understand what online messaging entails, the type of audience they constitute, and how transcendent it is to protect their privacy and respect for others on the Internet.

They live in an environment full of unwanted messages, where the motto "wherever you want, whenever you want" reigns. They are prosumers without being aware of it, in a virtual society where ubiquity is daily.

"The network becomes a gigantic virtual shopping center, stores that are open 24 hours a day 365 days a year, in all the countries that allow the full access of their citizens to it. From stores that sell everything: products, services, ideas, beliefs, contacts.

A shopping center where only a few customers understand which store they go to, while most, not to get lost, ask for help in a booth that says, search engines, -eight out of ten users looking to buy something in the net they do it through them. Customers who like to share their experiences in stores, and also tell them how good or bad they have been treated, so stores should keep an eye out." (Miranda Villalón et al., 2010, p. 17-18)

Prosumers, citizens, users, and others. No matter what term we use, the description we have given leads us to conclude that it is decisive to propose measures to implement media and digital literacy policies urgently.

In the article, "Is Google Making Us Stupid," the main point the author, Nicholas Carr (2008), wrote:

"I've had an uncomfortable sense that someone, or something, has been tinkering with my brain, remapping the neural circuitry, reprogramming the memory. My mind isn't going— so far as I can tell—but it's changing. I'm not thinking the way I used to think. I can feel it most strongly when I'm reading— immersing myself in a book or a lengthy article used to be easy. My mind would get caught up in the narrative or the turns of the argument, and I'd spend hours strolling through long stretches of prose. That's rarely the case anymore. Now my concentration often starts to drift after two or three pages. I get fidgety, lose the thread, begin looking for something else to do. I feel as if I'm always dragging my wayward brain back to the text. The deep reading that used to come naturally has become a struggle."

And it seems to be true. Interestingly, it had never been read or written as much as in the present era. According to data from 2017, in just one minute on the planet, 452,000 tweets are issued, or 156 million e-mails are sent, although many of them correspond to *spam* or *bot* products.

In parallel, today, according to specialists Roger Bohn and James Short (2009), in research, 27% of the information that people consume in a day comes from reading on the Internet.

That is a figure like what happened in the 80s with newspapers (26%), with which the data indicate that reading has not decreased, but the way to access it.

It should be noted that this was studied in the United States a decade ago, before the emergence of smartphones, which should increase the indicator.

These radical changes in behavior as readers or writers are often taken as a sign that we are in a change of era and that there are terrible and irreversible processes involved. But you do not have to go that fast. Nothing is as new as imagined. (Martínez, 2019)

Each of the cases mentioned is explained to the extent that it is noticed that reading and writing are *cognitive technologies,* as the researcher Andy Clark (1989) says. Changes in media, practices, in formats continually modify reading and writing cognition.

Think of the difference between writing on a parchment *versus Word,* where a typo on the parchment forces it almost to be discarded, while *Word* autocorrects.

Think also of Jack Kerouac's "the roll," that resource that the beatnik writer used to paste, one after another, many typewriter sheets that allowed him to write *On the Road* in one fell swoop of three weeks in April 1951 without having to change sheets every time he finished a flat.

This meant that this book was perceived as a continuous flow of language and not as separate sections. It is as if it were a single long paragraph, which conveys the vertigo of the newly released youth of the late forties in the United States.

Seen in this way, the fear that "Google will make us stupid" is anchored in more ancestral fears that accompanied personalities of the past as far away as St. Augustine of Hippo or, closer, characters like Baudelaire or Nietzsche, who already saw that the technologies of reading and writing changed the ways of doing things.

THE INTERNET IS NOT FREE

Technologies have always served the empowerment of citizens. It is worth remembering the emergence of the printing press. Although its initial objective was more of control by an elite of the society at the time, it became a revolutionary weapon for humanity.

Changes are being made in the second decade of the 21st century, the consequences of which are still tough to predict but will undoubtedly draw a hugely different landscape than we know so far. Although some are restricting themselves from so-called techno-optimistic thinking, ruling out the possibility that technologies include advances for the country, as is the case of a more significant and better democracy.

It is indisputable that they have served to mobilize peoples. Moreover, citizenship is confronting injustices and states of corruption through so-called digital democracy, which is a reality far from being utopian.

Citizens are exposed to an "informational nuclear explosion," such an expression used by Pérez Tornero (2012), about the new forms of communication that make us involved. That move our voice and which, as we have seen in the latest social events -Arab Spring, 15M Movements in Spain, and others- come to produce fundamental transformations in governments, states, and society.

The power that has taken over the Internet and, above all its users, provoke actions that can even be feared by the states themselves in the face of the possible loss of power. As Castells states: "Governments hate the Internet fundamentally because it is a basic challenge to what was always the foundation of their power: that is the control of information and communication."

As Peter Osnos wrote in *The Atlantic:*

"The mantra of a "free" Internet has shaped the prevailing view of how we access information and entertainment in the digital age. This enduring myth is actually a misnomer. It continues to obscure a serious problem faced by significant sectors of society unable to take full advantage of the Internet or meet the high price of cable and cellular phone systems that are at the core of today's personal technology... For all the progress in delivering information and entertainment in the Internet era, Americans deserve and should demand something closer to the ideal of what is possible with our technology. It is now well short of what it could be." (2013)

We must know that the unimaginable digital revolution that we are experiencing, which already touches so many activities and professions, has also wholly modified the field of information and surveillance. Surveillance has become omnipresent and immaterial, imperceptible, undetectable, and invisible in the Internet age. In addition, it is already, technically, of excessive simplicity.

With the impulse of consumption, "online" has developed considerably commercial-type surveillance, which has generated a massive market for personal data, turned into merchandise. (Ramonet, 2015)

When we do not connect to a website, the *cookies* store the set of the searches made in memory, establishing a new consumer profile. In an instant, the editor of the page we visit sells information that affects us to potential advertisers, collected all by the *Cookies.*

Some milliseconds after appearing on our screen, the advertising supposedly has more impact on us. And we are already defining ourselves.

Cyberspace has become a kind of the fifth element. The Greek philosopher Empedocles proposed that our world was formed by four parts: earth, air, water, and fire.

But the emergence of the Internet, with its mysterious "interspace," superimposed on ours, formed by thousands of millions of digital exchanges of all kinds.

Its *streaming* and *clouding* have engendered a new universe, in a particular quantum way, that will complete the reality of our contemporary world as an authentic fifth element.

The Internet has become centralized. At first, the Net was perceived as an explosion of possibilities of individual expression, which made it possible to escape from the dependence of the state monopoly (mail, telegraph, telephone), of the giants of the telecommunications, and the ample dominant means of communications (graphic press, radio, television).

It was synonymous with freedom, of evasion, of creativity. Yet, twenty-five years after, the Network is about to suffer a violent centralization around colossal private companies: the 'GAFAM' (Google, Apple, Facebook, Amazon, Microsoft), all Americans who, on a planetary scale, monopolize the different facets of the Network, and the ones that we are dependents on the approximately 3,500 million of internauts, who, in turn, feed them with all their date. And in this way, they enrich immensely.

Sometimes it may seem that this type of voice contagion is done spontaneously. However, it is prevalent to see how users of social networks and other media involvement learn their use in a self-taught and again, by contagion.

One thing is obvious, the use of these technologies can be a powerful tool for change, for the visibility of ideas, opinions, different voices that are heard. Perhaps what is needed is a higher impulse to teach how to manage them and use them from a critical point of view since they are equally powerful in unleashing adverse and harmful effects according to the wearer's intention.

In keeping with the above, Postman (1992), in his reflection on the Technopolis two decades ago, concluded that "technologies alter the structure of our interests: the things we think about, and they alter the nature of the community: the space in which thoughts develop" (p 33). This way of Postman understanding the world – it was the 90s – and interacting with it today requires higher and better knowledge management.

The power of the prosumer to which we refer may not be harnessed, exploited at its broadest conception, preventing the citizens from benefiting. Six years later, the same author stated: "Those who have control over the management of a particular technology accumulate power and inevitably shape a kind of conspiracy against those who do not have access to the specialized knowledge that the technology enables" (Postman, 1998, p 20).

This remains worrying as the technological gap between peoples – which continues to exist – becomes "the gap in participation." For Jenkins (2008), the participation gap makes it impossible for the acquisition of knowledge for vigilant citizens:

"The challenge lies not simply in the ability to read and write, but in the ability to participate in the deliberations on the issues and more relevant knowledge, and on the forms of knowledge that require authority and respect" (p 256).

The COVID-19 pandemic is unusual as it poses a challenge to the global socio-economic system. The phenomenon affects advanced economies and emerging countries alike to the extent that, both for its effects and the public policies put into practice, it represents a rethinking of social practices and productive systems considered standard until the end of last year.

In terms of telecommunications infrastructure and digital connectivity, the most precise indicators include the exponential increase in Internet traffic (and the consequent challenge for operators to preserve adequate quality levels), the importance of teleworking, and the need to maintain active supply and distribution chains of goods. (Agudelo et al., 2020)

In a document of the United Nations Commission for the economic development of Latin America and the Caribbean (CEPAL-UN), they wrote the conditions to use the digital tools to mitigate the effects of the Pandemic in the region:

1. "Can digitalization act as a mitigating factor, reducing the disruptive impact of the pandemic?
2. What is the degree of deployment of digital platforms to address the need to disseminate health control measures, facilitate consumer transactions and continue to educate children?
3. In the same way, can the Latin American productive system migrate to a context where supply chains are supported by the efficient flow of digital information?
4. To what extent can telecommunications networks respond to the challenge of a mass migration to teleworking?

5. Can the State continue to function from a digitalization of administrative and management processes?" (p 3)

Telecommunications infrastructure is critical to support today's economic and social actions. It is a robust, innovative, and changing infrastructure. Access to it, the internet, telecom services, and information technologies is a human right that enables the exercise of other fundamental rights such as health, education, culture, security, freedom of expression, and mobility, among others.

This infrastructure is strategic because, in critical situations such as the one faced against COVID-19, it preserves the exercise of these rights and is the best ally of governments and society to maintain the economy.

The personal experience of working on radio and television for 20 years and the stints as a War Correspondent in Indochina, Africa, and Central America, help me to understand the COVID challenges to teaching.

As I said in the Foreword is not a question of technology, but mentality. Previously exercising webcasts using *BC Collaborate, Zoom, WebEx Cisco,* and *Adobe Connections*, not counting *Skype, FaceTime, Facebook Messenger, Google Duo,* and others, was not all.

The most crucial part is combining the student participation and motivation, under the stress of the Pandemic and the lack of understanding or their loved ones -also under 'cabin fever'- that they were participating in a college class.

What shocked me the most was the illiteracy of the students, most of them *Millennials* and *Gen Z*, on the use of the Clouds, Wi-Fi for video, videotaping software, and other old digital systems, simple things that they were supposed to master as digital natives.

They had expensive smartphones, tablets, laptops, and computers for a thousand dollars. However, the knowledge of the network cards and roaming capabilities were beyond their comprehension.

It is not a new concept, as Baskakova and Soboleva (2019) of the *Russian Academy of Sciences* wrote:

"A pivotal trend in modern socioeconomic development is the active digitalization of the most diverse aspects of societal life marking the onset of the so-called digital economy [IMF

2018]. A country's ability to fit into this trend successfully is largely determined by the so-called "national human potential". The problem of adjusting this potential to the new requirements is multifaceted, the most obvious facet being the need for expanded reproduction of experts in information infra-structure creation and maintenance. Of no less importance, however, is how the people at large will adapt to the new reality." (p 244)

That's key: "how the people at large will adapt to the new reality." They mentioned the *UNESCO* (1978) Statistics of Illiteracy Definitions

"A person is functionally literate who can engage in all those activities in which literacy is required for effective functioning of his group and community and also for enabling him to continue to use reading, writing and calculation for his own and the community's development." (p 18)

Are they? Are our students, or what's worst, our academic and administrative personnel ready? Baskakova and Soboleva (2019) expand:

"In today's world, therefore, functional illiteracy acquires a considerably larger scale, affecting well-educated social groups with human capital of the pre-digital era who are unable to seamlessly fit into the new economic reality that requires mastering skills and technology adequate to the digital economy." (p 245)

Is it only a Russian problem? Experience tells us no. Or a report from the US Department of Education (Mademova, Pawlowski Hudson, 2018)

"Adults who are not digitally literate are, on average, less educated, older, and more likely to be Black, Hispanic, or foreign born, compared to digitally literate adults. Compared to digitally literate adults, adults who are not digitally literate have a lower rate of labor force participation and tend to work in lower skilled jobs.

Compared to adults internationally (i.e., in other OECD countries), a smaller proportion of U.S. adults are not digitally literate. About 16 percent of U.S. adults are not digitally literate, compared to 23 percent of adults internationally. The percentage of U.S. adults who are not digitally literate is not measurably different from the percentages in England/Northern Ireland (UK), Flanders (Belgium), Canada, and Germany. The Netherlands and several Nordic countries (Sweden, Norway, and Denmark) have some of the lowest percentages of adults who are not digitally literate, ranging from 11 to 14 percent.

Across the countries studied, 71 percent of adults use a computer at work and 83 percent of adults use a computer in everyday life. In comparison, 74 percent of U.S. adults use a computer at work, 3 percentage points higher than the international average, and 81 percent of U.S. adults use a computer in everyday life, 3 percentage points lower than the international average." (p 5)

However, it looks like the US Department of Education is not alone there. The PEW Research center coincides:

It doesn't look like a generational problem, as the sessions in Congress about social media showed: "The senators and the *Facebook* founder spoke different languages, and there was no simultaneous translation." (Sullivan, 2018)

"The hearing [about Facebook] should give everyone serious

pause if they think that federal legislation is going to solve the serious and growing issues of technology run amok.

For one simple reason: Legislators don't seem to understand it well enough to even ask the right questions, much less fix the problem … Sen. Bill Nelson (Fla.), the ranking Democrat on the Commerce Committee.

Nelson, 75, started out by stating his less-than-convincing digital bona fides: "From the moment we get up, we're on those handheld..." and here he paused, searching for the right word and finishing up with a flourish: ". . . tablets."

Sen. Charles E. Grassley (R-Iowa), 85, who ran Tuesday's show, strained over unfamiliar words as he asked Zuckerberg about "complex click-through consent pages."

And 84-year-old Sen. Orrin G. Hatch (R-Utah) tried his best but continued to call the largest tech platforms "websites," as if referring to Zappos.com. Then he teed up a question so basic about Facebook's business model that Zuckerberg answered it in four words: "Senator, we run ads."

That's not to say, of course, that there aren't plenty of people in their 70s and 80s who understand technology. The issue here is less about age than about familiarity and knowledge. (And undoubtedly some members of Congress are tech-savvy)."

Digital illiteracy appears as a ghost of the past. Its mission would be to remind society of the actions that have historically been undertaken to overcome traditional illiteracy, which has plunged entire peoples into silence for years.

Within traditional literacy, a category called functional illiteracy is contemplated. For example, the person capable of recognizing letters, signing, and reading small messages is functionally illiterate, but in practice, does not understand the content of the message exposed.

Digital illiteracy carries a disadvantage, being a product of the technocentrism surrounding it since its appearance. (Yépez-Reyes, 2018)

"Experts warn against the danger following passive consumption of the products of technologically advanced transformations, namely: shows, programmes, and applications. As a result of their extensive use, more and more children experience distorted sensory faculties, concentration difficulties, problems with listening, feeling emotions, or even navigating in their environment (Patzlaff, 2008). *Cyberdeseases*, include *digiilliteracy*, or linguistic difficulties of digital natives, which is one of the consequences of operating in a contemporary 'high-tech' world." (Lichtańska & Cygan, 2020, p 255)

We propose to design ways to use resources to integrate digital capabilities in our higher education centers. The budgets for the growth of facilities, maintenance, and gigantic administrative and employee departments can be allocated to this objective, not counting the reduction of onerous tuition costs for students and their families.

Empty libraries with expensive computer systems, buildings, and employees, are not a decision question. Still, they are the past in a world where you can have all the information you need to click on a digital tool.

However, we need to design programs to instruct our students and their families to use the systems they lack knowledge of and our personal in the academic and administrative field. If you lack the knowledge, you can not teach others to use them.

In previous centuries it was understood as literate to those who knew how to read and write. Today, where communication occurs through written language, the concept of literacy changes altogether.

At present, the domain of literacy alone seems insufficient since it only allows access to a part of the information conveyed in our society: that which is accessible through books.

A technologically illiterate person is left out of the communicative network offered by new technologies. From the above, we can deduce that digitally illiterate people develop their personal and professional activities without being linked to technologies or digital media. (Icaza-Álvarez et al., 2019, p 399)

Some general characteristics are a solid resistance to incorporating technologies into their different processes, validating traditional means as the only effective ones for the performance of their tasks.

The ability alone to handle technological tools and instruments, mobile phones, iPods, PCs, and others does not give the power to be a digital savvy person. It is possible to propose that basic skills, either making a presentation or writing a document with the computer's word processor, are not enough to overcome digital or technological illiteracy.

In our own experience, the resistance to learning from some of the must disadvantage students of minorities, or first-generation immigrants, come not only from the humiliation from their peers of inequality in society. But, principally, for the unacceptable ways of a system that accepts them -and their thousands of dollars of tuition- without adequate training in digital technologies.

Denying the possibilities of communicating is not only wrong, is also against the human rights of students and communities, or as Kaplún (1985) wrote almost three decades ago.

"True communication is not given by a speaker and a listener, but by two or more human beings or communities that exchange and share experiences, knowledge, feelings (even if at a distance through artificial means [or channels]. It is through that process of exchange that human beings establish relationships with each other and move from isolated individual existence to communal social existence... the communication process must be carried out in such a way as to give everyone the opportunity to be alternately senders and receivers. Defining what we mean by communication is equivalent to saying what kind of society we want to live in." (Kaplún, 1985)

Let us recap: digital or multimedia **literacy** refers to the skills needed to properly locate, understand, and analyze information through digital technologies, mastering all the tools at hand.

That is, the necessary skills that every person needs to be able to use and include technologies in their day-to-day before they must confront a class and the require daily use of technology to improve themselves.

Digital communication shaped how people interact with each other, form interest groups, and maintain their socialization. As a result, social networks became an integral part of modern life, generating new needs and establishing a unique frame to fulfill them. More than 37% of the globe's population engaged in different social media platforms in 2016 (Gallagher, 2017).

The *Digital 2020: Global Overview Report* revealed that 4.54 billion people currently enjoy the Web, whereas 3.80 billion are social media users (Kemp, 2020).

The Internet and social networks alter communication patterns and life aspects of around 60% of the world's population.

Nowadays, social media evolved into a life-changing and indispensable socio-cognitive interface that shapes the language and mode of interpersonal communications. Shortenings, novel words, changed meanings, and multimodality of discourse appear on *Tumblr* or *Facebook*. Moreover, social media users internalize in smaller social groups that guide their behavior.

Network society, self-determination, and social identity theories suggest that social networking meets an individual's most essential psychological needs. Although electronic discourse ignores some standard language norms, it is a natural dialectical development phase fostered by globalization rather than linguistic degradation.

IMPACT OF SOCIAL MEDIA ON SELF-DETERMINATION

Online communication has become an essential part of social life for every modern person. It changed the way people talk both in terms of quantity and quality. (Shakirovna, 2021) Many day-to-day tasks in life are unbearable without reaching others with social media. Although the Internet is compelling for users, it is crucial to determine its psychological nature and motivations.

The self-determination theory (S.D.T.) explains the human motivation to use *Facebook* and other networking mediums. This macro-theory, introduced by Edward L. Deci and Richard M. Ryan (2000, p. 237), states that individuals have an innate tendency to regulate behavior based on choice and interest. (Brichacek et al., 2018, p. 2)

All people's internal states are influenced by external (environmental and social) factors. Thus, motivation is "the interplay between internal states and external factors impacting those states" (Ferguson et al., 2015, p. 298). In other words, S.D.T. applies the concept of need satisfaction that explains why people are self-determined to join a particular activity.

According to Gila Cohen Zilka (2018) of *Bar-Ilan University*, Israel, they satisfy three basic psychological needs: competence, autonomy, and relatedness. (p. 1) The more people think that their needs are met in each domain, the greater chance they will assimilate and be accountable for their actions (Ferguson et al., 2015, p. 302). The positive outcomes related to need satisfaction include well-being, work satisfaction, and vitality.

The regulation of motivation is possible intrinsically and extrinsically by different forms of self-determination. The continuum of states ranges from inspiration to autonomous motivation, like when an external incentive impulses behavior in a particular way through implicit rewards and punishment, decreasing positive outcomes.

Autonomous motivation is related to a pleasure-based prosocial stance in the participation of the netsocieties, leading to well-being and self-actualization in our virtual communities. Although people are social species relying on cooperation, their nature includes autonomous decision-making over many life issues.

Social Media possesses the necessary characteristics to facilitate self-regulation and internalization over time. It creates an autonomy-supportive environment were users
can freely exchange content between participants, converse with others, and build various relationships. Ronald Ferguson and other researchers (Ferguson et al. 2015, p. 302) found that *Facebook* users express more excellent supportive intentions for charity when integrated regulation influences their motivation.

Integrated regulation of autonomous motivation occurs when individuals perceive their behavior as suitable to the sense of self. This means when one behaves following personal beliefs, values, prejudices, fears, preconceived ideas, role in our culture, and natural learning—just part of being humans.

Moreover, distinct types of social media that create room for collaboration (*Quora, Reddit*), relationships (*Facebook, WhatsApp*), and creativity (*YouTube, Pinterest*) fulfill human candidate needs. Yu-Qian Zhu and Houng-Gee Chen (2015) from the *National Taiwan University* consider them socially orientated and address relatedness. (p. 6)

They identify four everyday activities users perform: participating in shared activities, feeling appreciated and understood, participating in pleasant or otherwise enjoyable actions, and communicating about personally relevant matters (p. 4). These events meet the general need for relatedness, especially when people join online social groups with similar views and aspirations.

Henri Tajfel and John C. Turner (2004) proposed the social identity theory explains why people form and join groups based on shared beliefs and interests. They give a sense of social identity, belonging to a particular way of life, ideology, or religion. Human beings tend to stereotype others categorizing them as in-group and out-group. (p. 279)

Identifying differences and similarities to other assemblies of individuals is a natural cognitive process. Social identification is an interplay between internal and external comparisons or dialectic processes. Jillianne R. Code and Nicholas Zaparyniuk (2010) state that "the Internet enables individuals to develop and express multiple social identities and experiment with new virtual identities" (p. 1348). Modern human beings have multiple identities that help them adapt to various social contexts.

Communication in professional, cultural, functional, organizational, and other levels facilitates these social identities. Thus, for instance, a lawyer socializing online and offline can identify himself as a parent, advocate, or friend in different societal contexts without apparent conflict of interests.

To join a group, individuals undergo a self-categorization to associate themselves with specific social categories and identities (Code & Zaparyniuk, 2010, p. 1347). Then, the formed collective identity depersonalizes people, making them group members.

Modern communication technologies facilitate collective identification by enabling users to experiment with their virtual identities.

The network society is another critical theory developed by Barry Wellman, Manuel Castells, and Jan van Dijk, which gives insight into how Internet-based communication technologies influence socialization. This social formation depends on the infrastructure that shapes its prime mode of organization and essential structure at organizational, individual, and societal levels (Van Dijk, 2020, p. 336).

This concept opposes mass and information society claiming that the Internet brings together organizational, interpersonal, and mass communication. So, the perception of technology is a defining factor of the organizational structure, whereas political, cultural, and economic factors shape such societies' context. Thus, internet users link to one another and can communicate and exchange information regularly.

The network society creates a platform for small groups based on shared interests and beliefs that others can hear. However, today society pressures individuals to join social media sites and fit into specific social ones. For instance, it is not easy to imagine that the professional manager does not use instant messenger or social networks to stay connected with their staff. People turn to social media to receive acceptance from separate groups.

Ruotsalainen & Heinonen describe "a possible future, in which the network society is deepening to become an internet-based ecosystemic society. The study of the possible societal impacts of the 'media disruption' brought along by the internet has been somewhat neglected." (2015, p 8)

Furthermore, social networks help individuals acquire the necessary information and join groups of interest; they also change how Internet users behave and think. Markus Kaakinen and other researchers (Kaakinen et al., 2018) found an association between users' time in social media groups and their behavior's stability. According to them, members start to mimic the behavior of others following prolonged engagement. (p. 21)

Hence, social media platforms attract people with similar interests, whereas collective identity later shapes and reinforces it. A specific set of social viewpoints and rules guide members' behavior, including how they communicate with each other and society (Stocker & Bossomaier, 2014, p. 15).

For instance, a *Facebook* group of lawyers may apply common terminology and abbreviation in their posts that the out-group would hardly understand. Likewise, similar principles, backgrounds, ideologies, or intentions can influence how members converse, natural exercise among everyday humans.

Social networks and accompanied technical development changed the way we communicate. One of the main changes spotted by U.S. researcher Mandy Edwards (2015) is the sheer number of means to interact. Before the onset of such platforms as *Facebook*, people could interact mainly with individuals they know in person.

Nowadays, everybody who has access to the Internet and social network site accounts can share their thoughts, opinions, and beliefs with thousands of other users or group members. Thus, online networking contributes to globalization by allowing instant information exchange between various ethnicities, races, religions, and cultures.

The involvement of Netcitzens in discussion and assessment of their text or media contributions, either on the sites or smartphone applications, is, of course, determined by the situation, timing, and connection capabilities of the specific medium they use. As Marshall McLuhan wrote: "the medium is the message." (1964, p. 9)

What is more important, the Web influenced its users' writing techniques and discourse. As a result, a trend of summarized writing sees short messages with the exact meaning and intent. For instance, *Twitter* pioneered the 30-word limit, forcing people to choose the most appropriate to convey the core message (Edwards, 2015).

The users must report on their life events or share opinions in shorter sentences to comply. Consequently, people who communicate using instant messengers or social networks often neglect correct grammar or semantic usage. Emojis and various abbreviations form an entirely new language that other members commonly and easily understand, expanding to emotions, completed by the most recent 'memes.'

The interactivity of social media results in the proliferation of abbreviations and acronyms such as "btw," "lol," and "oic" for "oh, I see." Moreover, social networks are characterized by its effective discourse style "marked by a high degree of intensification – capitalization, repeated exclamation marks, repetition, exaggerated quantifiers, such as "all" and "everyone," and frequent use of boosters." (Darvin, 2016, p. 527)

This linguistic pattern of intensification emerges from users' intention to make their everyday stories more exciting and unique on social media.

Instead of facial expressions and gestures people use in face-to-face communication, they apply emoticons and images to convey the message. The Web users also turn to the lexicalization of vocal sounds, like "haha" or "umm;" the spelling of sounds, "coooool," "Kewl," and formulaic openings and closings (Darvin, 2016, p. 528).

Language loses its supremacy and importance in exchanging information due to digital storytelling that features different modes such as gestures, images, writing, speech, music, and 3D objects. According to Lauren Gawne and Gretchen McCulloch (2019), emojis parallel to bodily actions and facial expressions relates to accompanying text or speech. Text-accompanying emoticons' meaning can change by the context and have possible form variation.

Electronic discourse evolved into a new variety of the language with semi-speech writing features. Despite its popularity among young people, the research conducted by Atef Odeh AbuSa'aleek (2015) found that they can only classify 25% of students' words as an electronic language. (p. 136) It conflicts with a common notion that adolescents and young adults use a shortened incomprehensible code.

The e-discourse features included in language assessment comprises shortening, clippings, contractions, unconventional spellings, word-letter, word-digit replacements, word combinations, and initialisms. According to the findings, the most popular language e-communication feature is weird spelling, while the word combination almost remained untouched.

As Davis and Brewer (1997) wrote defining it:

"Electronic discourse is one form of interactive communication… Like any other way that humans use language for interaction and communicative purposes, electronic discourse is multifaceted and complex." (p 13)

They agree that it is not a 'surrogate for language' but a different context for its use.

MULTIMODALITY OF E-COMMUNICATION

The multimodality of discourse is one of the essential sociolinguistic changes brought by social media. Danica Jovanovic and Theo Van Leeuwen (2018) examined social media applying semiotic technology and social communication theories. According to them, social networks support a multimodal dialog if it through pre-designed templates of information exchange. (p. 689)

Social media use and design interdependence, with users responding to it within specific dialog forms: a functional exchange structure and evaluative correspondence guide the dialogue and cast task-orientated, conversational, and question-answering systems to regular conversations, mediatic or not. (Deriu et al., 2020, p. 3)

It partially explains why people alter their writings and respond with pictures or emoticons following dialogs on *Viber, Snapchat, Twitter*, or *Facebook*. By Michael Mehmet and other researchers (Mehmet et al., 2014), new media modalities make users employ various combinations to change or create new kinds of meanings. On the social media platforms, "language may be combined with visual, auditory, and kinetic resources, to construct very complex texts over time" (p. 4).

The Social Semiotic Multimodality framework states that users can understand social media messages based on meaning-making resources. Social media producers designed and provided such resources, informing consumers to use them and the theory of prosumers, consumers of their own produced product. (Toffler, 1980, p. 283)

Today, most posts and messages include different modalities perceived and understood through intersemiotic relations, as Roman Jakobson (1959) coined (in Giannakopoulou, 2019, p. 199). The intersemiotic framework suggests that enhancement, complementarity, or concurrence realized the meanings of messages. Concurrence occurs when clarifying a text, re-expressing it, or exemplifying with other modes help.

For instance, a picture exemplifies the post on *Facebook* containing the pie recipe. The second resource is complementarity, when one mode adds meaning to another (Mehmet, 2014, p. 5). The image can add new meaning to the text or even put image and text content at variance.

The third relation is the enhancement and occurs when an additional message multiplies the meaning already stated in another mode. Such an Internet phenomenon as memes can be a fitting example of enhancement, as text usually creates the condition, while an image is the event's outcome.

The formation of online groups is contingent on interests or social features that often share the specific knowledge that influences their speaking and writing. For example, some content creators on *YouTube* mention the terminology of games, medicine, film, or the beauty industry in their videos. However, those who face it for the first time can hardly comprehend it, whereas their subscribers understand many covered notions. In their turn, social networks created for texting and sending voice messages are limited to add to such effect due to imposed rules of behavior, word limits, and website design.

It forms a socio-cognitive interface that dictates norms and models of language use. The more individuals integrate into the group, the more they concur linguistically to fit the online environment. Language is a necessity for human existence, as a participating phenomenon of societies to communicate or distribute information,

Moreover, digital communication fosters translingual practices when people often mix lingo or continually code-switching. Transnational relations, migration process, and social media communication enabled the process of "textual co-construction, collaborative meaning-making and different types and degrees of language mixing" (Darvin, 2016, p. 529).

As a result, individuals who simultaneously apply separate languages tend to use uncommon words and idioms. Users of the same online social group would understand this new code-meshed linguistic synergy. As Charles K. Ogden and Igor A. Richards (1923) wrote: "sometimes the disputants are using the same words for different things, sometimes different words for the same things."

(Ogden, 1945, p. viii)

Adolescents and young adults are more eager to endorse such written and verbal communication changes due to their excessive need for self-determination. They naturally perceive it as slang that makes them different from their parents, who belong to previous generations. On the contrary, representatives of prior generations may characterize this phenomenon as an inferior way to communicate, a sign of illiteracy.

However, the idea of literacy as a pre-constructed element of local cultural systems is outdated and needs revision. For example, Dr. Suresh Canagarajah advocates the need for a negotiated literacy model instead of conventional situate literacy (2013, p. 43; in Darvin, 2016, p. 529). Furthermore, language alterations on the Internet do not depend on grammar, punctuation, and formal semantics standard for face-to-face interactions.

The world of digital communication forces people to adapt and learn how to use the new form of language to be successful in the online aspect of socialization. According to the network society's core ideas, interaction change is a natural process ignited by technology development.

The skills needed to comprehend and reply to messages on the Web now are highly important. When formal offline communication still requires literacy in its original meaning because literacies are the center of social networking. Hence, it is not enough in network societies to know how to read and speak in real life; it is also essential to be effective on the Web.

CONCLUSIONS

To conclude, the advent of modern technologies encouraged social networking to apply digital ways of communication. As a result, human beings strive for autonomous decision-making and social acceptance. According to self-determination theory, individuals seek to fulfill their basic needs, including competence, autonomy, and relatedness.

Social network platforms provide their users with an autonomy-supportive environment that successfully addresses their relatedness needs. Integrated regulation of motivation to join the social media group creates the strongest associations with the cluster beliefs. Social identity theory shows how individuals undergo a self-categorization to internalize with in-group members.

People who form or join a specific online group with a social, ethnic, interest, or professional background usually change how they behave and speak or write. Ideologies or social believe firsthand experiences play an essential role in shaping the digital communication between humans.

In their turn, social networks set up pre-designed templates of information exchange that encourage users to alter how they communicate. The specific design affects the way people respond and conduct their dialogs. In general, E-discourse is not an incomprehensible mixture of acronyms and emoticons; it is instead an entirely new language. The main alterations made to the writings are unconventional spellings, word-digit replacements, word combinations, shortening, clippings, and contractions.

Social media also supports digital multimodal communication, characterized by the simultaneous use of various modes that create original meaning. Emojis, images, and 3D objects supplement the text with sentimentality and elicit emotions usually expressed by gestures and facial expressions. E-language is a new separate phenomenon that became a new standard of literacy.

As Lawrence of Arabia said: "Nothing is written." (O'Toole, 1962)

References

Abelson, H., Sussman, G. J. & Sussman, J. (1996). *Structure and Interpretation of Computer Programs*. foreword by Alan J. Perlis New York, NY: McGraw-Hill Book Company. https://web.mit.edu/alexmv/6.037/sicp.pdf

AbuSa'aleek, A. O. (2015). Internet Linguistics: A Linguistic Analysis of Electronic Discourse as a New Variety of Language. *International Journal of English Linguistics,* 5(1), 135-145. Doi: 10.5539/ijel.v5n1p135. https://www.academia.edu/103636 64/In ternet_Linguistics_A_Linguistic_Analysis_of_Electro nic_Discourse_ as _a_New_Variety_of_Language

Adami, E. (2017, Jan). Multimodality. DOI: 10.13140/RG.2.1. 4818.0565. In García, Ofelia, Flores, Nelson & Spotti, Massimiliano, Eds. *The Oxford Handbook of Language and Society.* Chapter 22, pp. 451-472 . https://www.academia.edu/188532 13/Multimodality

Adler, P. S. (2008). Technological Determinism. In Clegg, Stewart R & Bailey, James R., eds. (2008). *The International Encyclopedia of Organization Studies*, pp. 1528-39. https://www.marshall.usc.edu/sites/default/files/padler/intellcont/revisingTechnological%20Determinism-1.doc

Agudelo et al. (2020, Apr) Las oportunidades de la digitalización en Amé rica Latina frente al Covid-19 Naciones Unidas, 2020 CEPAL, CAF. https://repositorio.cepal.org/bitstream/handle/11362/45360 /4/OportDigitalizaCovid-19_es.pdf

Alshenqeeti, H. (2016). Are Emojis Creating a New or Old Visual Lan guage for New Generations? A Socio-semiotic Study. *Advances in Language and Literary Studies*, 7(6), 56-69. https://files.eric.ed.gov/fulltext/EJ1126897.pdf

Aguilar Edwards, A., Castellanos Cerda, V. & Perez-Salazar, G., Eds.

(2013, Jun). La producción del conocimiento en las ciencias de la comunicación y su incidencia social [The Production of Knowledge in the Sciences of Communication and Its Social Impact]. https://gabrielperezsalazar.files.word press.com/2013/06/20130 607-libro-colectivo-amic-2012-final.pdf

Aced, C. et al. (2009a). Visibilidad y viralidad. [Visibility and virality]. In: Vi sibilidad: cómo gestionar la reputación en Internet. [Visibility: How to manage reputation on the Internet]. Barcelona, Spain: *Gestión 2000*, p 83–102.

Aced, C. et al. (2009b). Las redes sociales. [The Social Networks]. In: [Vi sibility: How to manage reputation on the Internet]. Barcelona, Spain: *Gestión 2000*, p. 65–81.

Ahmad, N. (2019, Sep 12). The influence of technology on our daily lives https://hustlersdigest.com/the-influence-of-technology-on-our-dai ly-lives/

Albors, J., Ramos, J. C. & Hervas, J. L. (2008): New learning network pa radigms: Communities of objectives, crowdsourcing, wikis and open source. *International Journal of Information Management*, 28(3): 194-202.

Alcántara Plá, M. (2016). Neologismos Tecnológicos y Nuevos Compor tamientos [Technological Neologisms And New Behaviours]. In *La Sociedad Red*, Luis Gómez Encinas ed. Universidad Autóno ma de Madrid, España. *Aposta*. Revista de Ciencias Sociales, núm. 69: 14-38. https://www.redalyc.org/journal/4959/4959524 31002/html/#fn10

Álvarez Mellado, E. (2018, Nov 28). Baia baia. La irreverencia ortográfi ca del meme [The spelling irreverence of the meme]. Madrid, Spain: *El Mundo* newspaper. [Web Page]. https://www.eldiario .es/opinion/zona-critica/baia-baia-irreverencia-ortografica-me me_129_1812800.html

Anderson, J. & Rainie, L. (2018, Jun). Stories From Experts About the Impact of Digital Life. *PEW Research Center*. https://www.pewresearch.org/internet/2018/07/03/the-negatives-of-digital-life/

Androutsopoulos, J. (2011). Language change and digital media: a review of conceptions and Evidence. In Coupland, Nik & Kristiansen, Tore, eds. (2011). *SLICE: Critical perspectives on language (de)standardisation. Standard Languages and Language Standards in a Changing Europe*, pp. 145-160. https://pdfs.semanticscholar.org/1263/ce1d449c87c624687 d755f6fa8dd02f2dd6d.pdf

Androutsopoulos, J. (2015). *Towards a 'third wave' of digital discour se studies: audience practices on Twitter.* Ponencia presentada en la *1ˢᵗ International Conference Approaches to Digital Discourse Analysis* (ADDA). Valencia, 18-20 de noviembre de 2015.

Angenot, M. (1998). *Interdiscursividades. De hegemonías y disiden cias [Interdiscursiveness. of hegemonies and dissents]*. Córdoba, Argentina: Editorial Universidad Nacional de Córdoba. https://cursounneherasfadycc .files.wordpress.com/2011/10 /ange not-marc-interdiscursividades-de-hegemonias-y-diside ncias-1999.pdf

Arafah, B., Hasyim, M., & Kapoyos, F. E. (2021). E-democracy and the parrhesia language of netizen towards COVID-19 pandemic. *Linguistics and Culture Review*, 5(S1): 422-438. http ://www.lingcure.org/index.php/journal/article/view/1428/175

Arango Pinto, L. G. (2015). Una aproximación al fenómeno de los memes en Internet: claves para su comprensión y su posible integración pedagógica. [An approach to the phenomenon of memes on the Internet: keys to their understanding and their possible pedagogical integration]. *Comunicação, Mídia e Consumo*, 12, pp. 110-132. http://revistacmc.es m.br/index.php/revistacmc/article/view/677

Atton, C. (2015). *The Routledge Companion to Alternative and Community Media*, 1st ed. London, UK: Routledge Publishers.

Ávalos, P., Rivero, M. & Vigouroux, L. (2011). McLuhan y redes so ciales. In Valdettaro, Sandra Ed. (2011). *McLuhan. Pliegues, Trazos y Escrituras-post* (pp. 265-267). http://es.scribd.com/ tlatl/ d/76789612-eBook-McLuhan-Pliegues-Trazos-y-Escrituras-post-2 https://rephip.unr.edu.ar/bits tream/ handle/2133 /2021/ebook_mcluhan._pliegues__trazos_y_escrituras-post .pdf?sequence=1&isAllowed=y

Ayala Pérez, T. (2018, Aug 22). Del texto al hipertexto, del discurso al discurso multimodal: una mirada desde la cibercultura [From text to hypertext, from discourse to multimodal discour se: a look from cyberculture]. *Extos: Estudios de Humanidades y Ciencias Sociales*, (41). http://revistas.umce.cl/index. php/contextos/article/view/1398

Baeza-Yates, R. & Rello, L. (2011). How bad do you spell? The lexi cal quality of social media. In Nicolov, Nicolas & Shanahan, James G. (2011- Jul 17-21). *Proceedings of the 5th International AAAI Conference on Weblogs and Social Media: The Future of the Social Web Workshop* (ICWSM'11), p. 2-5. https://www.superarladislexia.org/p df/2011-Baeza-Yates% 20Rello-Social%20Media-icwsm-fosw.

Bancal, D. et al. & Ogez, E., coord. (2009). Cultivez votre identité nu mérique. [Cultivate your naked identity numeric]. http://issuu.

com/geemik/docs/cultivez_votre_identite_numerique

Baque Fajardo, I. A. (2018, Nov). *Análisis del uso de neologismos, acrónimos, Memes y emojis en la era digital* [Analysis of the use of Neologisms, Acronyms, memes and emojis in the digital age]. Bachelor's thesis Graphic Design and Advertising. Guayas, Ecua-dor: University of Milagro. http://repositorio. unemi.edu.ec/xmlui/handle/ 123456789/4257

Barlow, J. P. (2020, Jul 4). Una declaración de la independencia del ciberespacio by Fededav. https://blackswanfinances.com/ john-perry-barlow-una-declaracion-de-la-independencia-del-ciberespacio/

Barrett-Maitland, N. & Lynch, J. (2020, Feb 5). Social Media, Ethics and the Privacy Paradox, Security and Privacy From a Legal, Ethical, and Technical Perspective. IntechOpen, DOI: 10.5772/intechopen.90906. https://www.intechopen.com/ch apters/70973

Baron, N.S. (2009). *The Myth of Impoverished Signal: Dispelling the Spoken-Language Fallacy for Emoticons in Online Communi cation.* London: Peter Lang.

Baruah, T. D. (2012, May). Effectiveness of Social Media as a tool of communication and its potential for technology enabled connections: A micro-level study. *International Journal of Scientific and Research Publications*, 2(5): 1-10. http://www. ijsr p.org/research_paper_may2012/rp24.html#citation

Baskakova, M. & Soboleva, I. (2019, Jan). New Dimensions of Func tional Illiteracy in the Digital Economy. *Educational Studies Moscow.* 1, 244–263. DOI: 10.17323/1814-9545-2019-1-244 -263. https://cyberleninka.ru/article/n/new-dimensions-of-fun nctional-illiteracy-in-the-digital-economy/viewer

Baumer, M. & van Rensburg, H. (2011). Cross-Cultural Pragmatic Failure in Computer-Mediated Communication. *Coolabah*, 5, Observatori: Centre d'Estudis Australians, Australian Studies Centre, Universitat de Barcelona. http://www.ub.edu/dpfilsa /4baumervanrensburgcoola5.pdf

Bawden, D. (2008). Origins and Concepts of Digital Literacy. In C. Lankshear y M. Knobel (Eds.), *Digital Literacies: Concepts, Policies, and Practices* (pp. 17-32). New York: Peter Lang

Beltrán, R. E. (2017). Intervención de Procesos Mentales en la Es critura Digital en la Aplicación Whatsapp [Mental Process Intervention in Digital Writing in the Whatsapp application]. Master Thesis. Bogota, Colombia: Universidad Pedagógica Nacional. http://repository.pedagogica.edu.co/bitstream/han dle/20.500.12209/9902/TO-22009 .pdf?sequence=1&is Allowed=y

Blitvich, Pilar & Bou-Franch, Patricia. (2019). Introduction to Analyz ing Digital Discourse: New Insights and Future Directions: New Insights and Future Directions. 10.1007/978-3-319-926 63-6_1.

Benveniste, E. (1966), La philosophie analytique et le langage, in *Problèmes de linguistique générale*, vol. I, Paris: Gallimard, 267–276.

Berger, J. M. (2015, Aug). The Metronome of Apocalyptic Time So cial Media as Carrier Wave for Millenarian Contagion. Perspectives on Terrorism, 9(4), Special Issue on the Islamic State, pp. 61-71. https://www.jstor.org/stable/26297415

Bhana, Y. (2016, Apr 8). How Closed Societies Develop Anti-Lan gauges. https://www.translatemedia.com/us/blog-us/closed-societies-develop-anti-languages/

Birkerts, S. (2015). Changing the Subject. Minneapolis, Graywolf Press

Blackmore, S. (2000). The Meme Machine. Oxford, UK: Oxford University Press.

Blank, T. J., Ed. (2009). Folklore and the Internet: Vernacular Expression in a Digital world. Logan, Utah: Utah State University Press. https://digitalcommons.usu.edu/ cgi/viewcontent.cgi? article=1034& context=usupress_pubs

Bogost, I. (2019, Feb 11). Emoji Don't Mean What They Used To. *The Atlantic*, magazine [Web Page]. https://www.the atlantic.com/technology/archive/2019/02/how-new -emoji-are-changing-pictorial-language/582400/

Bolander, B., & Locher, M. A. (2014). Doing sociolinguistic research on computer-mediated data: A review of four methodological issues. *Discourse, Context & Media*, 3, 14-26. doi:10.1016/j. dcm.2013.10.004

Bolter, Jay David & Grusin, Richard (2000). *Remediation. Under standing New Media*. Cambridge, MA: MIT Press. https:/we/ monoskop.org/images/a/ae/Bolter_Jay_David _Grusin_Ri chard_Remediation_Understanding_New_Media_low_qualit y.pdf

Bohn, Roger & Short, James. (2009). How Much Information? 2009 Report on American Consumers. https://www.researchgate. net/publication/242562463_How_Much_Information_2009_ Report_on_American_Consumers

Brichacek, A., Neill, J., & Murray, K. (2018). The effect of basic psy chological needs and exposure to idealized Facebook images on university students' body satisfaction. *Cyberpsycho- logy: Journal of Psychosocial*

Research on Cyberspace, 12(3), 1-12. DOI: 10.5817/CP201 8-3-2. https://cyberpsychology.eu/article/view/11417/10176

Bronner, S. J. (2009). Digitizing and Virtualizing Folklore. In Blank, Trevor J., Ed. (2009). *Explaining Traditions. Folklore and the Internet: Vernacular expression in a digital world.* Chapter 1, pp. 21-6

Bronner, S. J. (2011). *Explaining Traditions: Folk Behavior in Mod ern Culture. Vernacular expression in a digital world* Lexington, KY: University Press of Kentucky

Bronner, S. J. (2011). *Virtual Tradition: On the Internet as a Folk System.* Kentucky Scholarship Online. DOI: 10.5810/kentucky/9780813134062.003.0011

Brooke, H. (2016). Inside the Digital Revolution. *Journal of Interna tional Affairs*, 70(1), pp. 29-53, 10. https://core.ac.uk/ download/pdf/82917227.pdf

Bryson, L., ed. (1948). *The Communication of Ideas.* New York: The Institute for Religious and Social Studies.

Bustos Martínez, L., De Santiago Ortega, P. P., Martínez Miró, M. Á. & Rengifo Hidalgo, M. S. (2019). Discursos de odio: una epidemia que se propaga en la red. Estado de la cuestión sobre el racismo y la xenofobia en las redes. [Hate Speech: an Epidemic That Spreads Online. State of Play on Racism and Xenophobia on Social Media]. Universidad Complutense de Madrid.

Bustos Reyes, C. (2016). El uso de los memes como lenguaje y/o forma de comunicación por jóvenes que cursan la enseñan za media en Santiago de Chile [The use of memes as language and/or form of communication by young middle scho ol in Santiago, Chile]. Santiago, Chile: *Universidad*

Finis Terrae. https://www.academia.edu/36 422276/El_uso_ de_ los _ memes_como_lenguaje_y_o_forma_de_comunicaci%C3 %B3n_ por_j%C3%B3venes_que_cursan_la_ense%C3%B 1anza_media_en_Santiago_de_Chile

Buettner, R. (2016): Personality as a predictor of business social media usage: An empirical investigation of XING usage pa tterns. *PACIS 2016 Proceedings.* June 27-July 1, Chiayi, Taiwan.

Byron, K.K. & Baldridge, D. (2007). E-Mail Recipients' Impressions of Senders' Likability: The Interactive Effect of Nonverbal Cues and Recipients' Personality. *Journal of Business Com munication,* 44(2): 137-160

Calvo Pérez, J. (2018, Jul 15). *El lenguaje en espacios virtuales* [Language in virtual spaces]. Lima, Peru, Universidad de San Martín de Porres de Lima https://www. uv.es/~calvo/ amerindias/Julio-Calvo-Lenguaje-Redes-Sociales.pdf

Canagarajah, S. (2013, Aug). Negotiating translingual literacy: an enactment. *Research in the Tea- ching of English,* 48(1), 40–67. https://www.jstor.org/stable/24398646?seq=1

Candale, C. V. (2017). Las características de las redes sociales y las posibilidades de expresión abiertas por ellas. La comu nicación de los jóvenes españoles en Facebook, Twitter e Instagram [The Features of social media and the Possibilities of expression by them. The communication of young Spaniards on Facebook, Twitter and Instagram]. *Colindancias: Revista de la Red de Hispanistas de Europa Central,* 8: 201-218. https://dialnet.unirioja.es/servlet/articulo?codi go=6319192

Canizzaro, S. (2016). Internet memes as internet signs: A semiotic view of digital culture. *SignSystems Studies,* 44(4): pp 562–586. https://www.researchgate.net/publication/312509193_ Internet_memes_as_internet_signs_A_semiotic_ view_of_ digital_culture

Camenisch et al. (2009). Blind and anonymous identity-based en cryption and authorised private searches on public key encrypted data. *Lecture Notes In Computer Science*, 5443.

Campbell, H. (2005). Considering spiritual dimensions within com puter-mediated communication studies. *New Media Society*, 7: 110–134.

Carr, N. (2008, Jul-Aug). Is Google Making Us Stupid? *The Atlan tic*, magazine [Web Page]. https://www.theatlantic. com/ ma gazine/archive/2008/07/is-google-making-us-stupid/306868

Carrión Martínez, P. S. (2015). *La Multimedia como herramienta de comprensión y visualización de estructuras relacionales del pensamiento complejo* [Multimedia as a tool of unders tanding and visualization of relational structures of complex thinking]. Master Thesis, Cuenca, Ecuador: Universidad del Azuay. http://201.159.222.99/ handle/ datos/5152

Carvajal Bello, M. A. & Chávez Pinzón, I. T. (2015). *El gesto ocul to: El silencio de la comunicación* [The hidden gesture: The silence of Communication]. Thesis for Social Communication. Bogotá, Colombia, Pontificia Universidad Javeriana. https://repository.javeriana.edu.co/handle/10554/19931

Chavero Ramírez, P., López-López, P. C., Puentes-Rivera, I. & Rocha, Á. (2018, Nov 18). Medios, Tecnologías Aplicadas y Comunicación [Media, Applied Technologies and Communication]. Editorial. *RISTI*, E16, Special Ed. Iberian Jou rnal of Information Systems and Technologies.

http://www. risti.xyz/issues/ristie 18.pdf and index
http://www.risti.xyz/
index.php?option=com_content&view=article& id=23&Item
id=122&lang=pt

Chen, Y. & Xie, J. (2008). Online consumer review: Word-of-mouth as a new element of marketing communication mix. *Mana Gement Science*, 54(3): 477-491.

Church, K., Ferreira, D., Banovic, N. & Lyons, K. (2015). Unders tanding the Challenges of Mobile Phone Usage Data. In Proceedings of the 17th International Conference on Human-Computer Interaction with Mobile Devices and Servi ces - *MobileHCI '15*. ACM Press, New York, New York. DOI: http://dx.doi.org/10.1145/2785830.2785891

Clark. (2017). Image Kerouac: On the Roll 2017 10. https://earthly mission.com/kerouac-on-the-roll/

Clark, A. (2004, Aug 31). Emoji: the first truly global language? *The Guardian* newspaper. https://www.theguardian.com/ techno logy/2014/aug/31/emoji-became-first-global-language

Clark, A. (1989). *Microcognition*. MIT Press. https://www.nyu.edu/ gsas/dept/philo/courses/concepts/clark.html

Clegg, S. R. & Bailey, J. R., eds. (2008). *The International Ency clopedia of Organization Studies*. Thousand Oaks, CA: Sage Publications.

Code, J. R., & Zaparyniuk, N. E. (2010). Social identities, group formation, and the analysis of online communities. https ://www. researchgate.net/publication/256297275_Social_ identities_ group_formation_and_analysis_of_online_com munities_Reprint. In S. Dasgupta (Ed.) *Social computing:*

Concepts, methodologies, tools, and applications (pp. 1346-1361). Informa tion Science Reference, an Imprint of I.G.I. Global.

Cognitive (2019, Sep 17). In Merriam-Webster's collegiate dictiona ry. [Web Page]. https://www.merriam-webster.com/dictio nary/cognitive Coupland, Nik & Kristiansen, Tore, eds. (2011). *SLICE: Critical perspectives on language (de) standardisa tion. Standard Languages and Language Standards in a Changing Europe*. Oslo, Norway: No vus. pp. 145-160. https: //pdfs.semanticscholar.org/1263/c e1d449c87c6 246 87d755f 6fa8dd02f2dd6d.pdf

Cole, N. L. (2020, Jan 24). Definition of Base and Superstructure Core Concepts of Marxist Theory. https://www.thoughtco. com/definition-of-base-and-superstructure-3026372

Compaine, B. M., Ed. (2001). *The Digital Divide Facing a Crisis or Creating a Myth?* https://mitpress.mit.edu/books/digital-divi de

Corey, A. M. (2009). Introducing Communication. In Tess Pierce ed *The* Evolution of Human Communication: from Theory to Practice. EtrePress. https: //ecampusontario.pressbooks. pub/evolutionhumancommunication/front-matter/the-evol ution-of-human-communication/

Cortés, F. (2006, Feb 6). Esclavos de las palabras. *ABC Madrid*. https://www.abc.es/opinion/abci-esclavos-palabras-200606 020300-1421833564446_noticia.html?ref=https%3A%2F% 2Fwww.google.com%2F

Crowell, S. (2017, Winter). Existentialism. *The Stanford Encyclope dia of Philosophy*. Edward N. Zalta, ed. [Web Page]. https:/ /plato.stanford.edu/archives/win 2017/entries/existentialism

Croft, W. & A. Cruse. (2004). *Cognitive Linguistics*. Cambridge, Cambridge University Press.

Crystal, D. (2003). *English as a global language*, 2nd ed. New York, NY: *Cambridge University* Press. http://www.cultural diplomacy.org/academy/pdf/research/books/nation_brandin g /English_As_A_Global_Language_-_David_Crystal.pdf

Crystal, D. (2006). *The Cambridge Encyclopedia of Language*, 3rd ed. Cambridge, UK: Cambridge University Press.

Crystal, D. (2006). Pragmatics. The factors that govern our choice of language in social Interaction; speech acts and their ana lysis; effect of the Internet. In Crystal, David (2006). *The Ca mbridge Encyclopedia of Language*, 3rd ed., pp. 124-128.

Crystal, D. (2002). *El lenguaje e Internet* [Language and the Inter net]. Madrid, Spain: Cambridge University Press.

Crystal, D. (2004). Language and the Internet, 2nd ed. Cambridge, UK: Cambridge University Press. http://medicine.kaums.ac. ir/upload edfiles/files/language_and_ %20the_internet.pdf

Cuadrado Gordillo, I., Martín-Mora Parra, G. & Fernández Antelo, I. (2015). La expresión de las emociones en la Comunicación Virtual. [The Expression of Emotions in the Virtual Co mmunication]. *El Ciberhabla*, Icono 14(13): 180-207. Doi: 10.7195/ri14.v13i1.716. https://dialnet.unirioja.es/descarga /articulo/4997133.pdf

Cupach, W. R., & Spitzberg, B. H. (Eds.). (1994). LEA's communi cation series. The dark side of interpersonal communication. Hillsdale, NJ, US: Lawrence Erlbaum Associates, Inc.

Czitrom, D. J. (1982). *Media and the American Mind: From Morse to McLuhan*. Chapel Hill, NC: Univ. of North Carolina Press.

Darics, E. (2010). Politeness in computer-mediated discourse of a virtual team. *Journal of Politeness Research*, 6(1): 129-150. Doi: 10.1515/jplr.2010.007

Darwin, C. (1889). *The descent of man and selection in relation to sex: with illustrations*. New York, NY: D. Appleton and Com pany. http://darwin-online.org.uk/ converted/pdf/1889_ Descent_F969.pdf

Dasgupta, S., Ed. (2009, Nov 30). *Social computing: Concepts, methodologies, tools, and applications*. 1st ed. Information Science Reference, an Imprint of I.G.I. Global.

Darvin, R. (2016). Language and identity in the digital age. https://www.researchgate.net/publicati on/303838217_Language _and_identity_in_the_digital_age. In S. Preece (Ed.). *The Rout- ledge Handbook of Language and Identity*. Routledge.

Davis, B. H., & Brewer, J. P. (1997). Electronic Discourse: Linguis tic Individuals in Virtual Space. Albany, NY: State Universi ty of New York Press.

Dawkins, R. (1989) *El gen egoísta: Las bases biológicas de nuestra conducta* [The selfish gene: The biological basis of our beha vior]. Barcelona, Spain: Biblioteca Científica Salvat.

Dawkins, R. (2006). *The selfish gene*. Oxford, UK: Oxford University Press. https://naturwissenschaftscafe.files.wordpress.com/ 2016/12/richard_dawkins_the_selfish _gene.pdf

DelReal, J. A. (2017, Nov 26). Trump Draws Scornful Rebuke fo Mocking Reporter with Disability. *The Washington Post*. http://www.washingtonpost.com/news/post-politics/wp/2015 /11/25/trump-blasted-by-new-yorktimes-after-mocking-repor ter-with-disability/?utm_term=.7ed1cb6de6a9

Deci, E. L. & Ryan, R. M. (2000) The "what" and "why" of goal pur suits: Human needs and the self-determination of behavior. *Psychological Inquiry*, 11(4), 227-268. DOI: 10.12 07/S1 5327965PLI1104_01

Deriu, J., Rodrigo, A., Otegi, A., Echegoyen, G., Rosset, S., Agirre E. & Cieliebak, M. (2020, Jun 25). Survey on evaluation me thods for dialogue systems. Artificial Intelligence Review. DOI: 10.1007/s10462-020-09866-x. https://link.springer.com/ article/10.1007/s10462-020-09866-x

Dijsselbloem, J. (2018, Jun 5). Towards a global language policy for emoji? An analysis of emoji as an evolving language. *Diggit Magazine*. Tilburg, The Netherlands: Tilburt University [Web Page]. https://www.diggitmagazine.com/papers/towards-glo bal-language-policy-emoji

Donsbach, W. (2008). *The international encyclopedia of communi cation*. Malden, MA: Blackwell Publications.

Dowerah Baruah, T. (2012, May). Effectiveness of Social Media as a tool of communication and its potential for technology enabled connections: A micro-level study. *International Journal of Scientific and Research Publications*, 2(5). http://www.ijsrp .org/research_paper_may2012/ijsrp-may-2012-24.pdf

Dudeney, G., Hockly, N. & Pegrum, M. (2013). *Research and Re sources in Language Teaching: Digital Literacies*. Harlow, UK: Pearson Publishers.

ECRI. (2014). Hate speech and violence. *European Commission against Racism and Intolerance* (ECRI). https://www.coe.int /en/web/european-commission-against-racism-and-intoleran ce/hate-speech-and-violence and https://rm.coe.int/ecri-gene ral-policy-recommendation-no-15-on-combating-hate-speec h/16808b5b01

Editorial Board (2016, Sep 25). Why Donald Trump Should Not Be President. *The New York Times*. http://www.nytimes.com/20 16/09/26/opinion/why-donald-trumpshould-not-be-president. html.

Edwards, M. (2015, Mar 17). How social media has changed how we communicate. FOW, *Future of Work*, Broadsuite Media Group. https://fowmedia.com/social-media-changed-commu nicate/

Ekman, P. (2004) Emotions revealed: Understanding faces and feeli ngs to improve communication and emotional life. Estados Unidos: Henry Holt and Co. https://zscalarts.files.wordpress. com/2014/01/emotions-revealed-by-paul-ekman1.pdf

El Ouirdi, M. E., El Ouirdi, A., Segers, J. & Henderickx, E. (2014, May 30). Social Media Conceptualization and Taxonomy: A Lasswellian Framework. Doi: 10.1177/0973258 614528608. *Journal of Creative Communications,* 9(2), 107-126. https:// www.researchgate.net/publication/262891233_Social_Media _Conceptualization_and_Taxonomy_A_Lasswellian_ Fra mework

Esparza Hernández, C. A. & Padierna Beltrán, A. (2018). La humani zación de los Discursos digitales [The Humanization of Digital Speeches]. In Herrero Gutiérrez, Francisco Javier et al., Eds. (2018). *Comunicación y música: mensajes, manifestaciones y negocios* [Communication and music: Messages, Manifestations and Business]. http://www.revistalatinacs .org/ 18SLCS/2018_libro2/002_Esparza.pdf

Fadel, C., Bialik, M. & Trilling, B. (2015). *Educación en Cuatro Di mensiones*. [Education in Four Dimensions]. Centro para el

Boston, MA: Rediseño Curricular. https://curriculumredesign
.org/wp-content/uploads/Educacion-en-cuatro-dimensiones-
Spanish.pdf

Fairclough, N. (1992). *Discourse and social change.* Cambridge:
Polity Press.

Farwell, J. P. (2012, Nov 27). *Persuasion and Power, The Art of
Strategic Communication.* Foreword by John J. Hamre.
Washington, DC: Georgetown University Press.

FCPolitUNR (2011, Aug 3) Mario Carlón en las Jornadas McLuhan
2011. [Mario Carlón at the McLuhan Days 2011]. [YouTube
Video]. http://www.youtube.com/ watch?v=2OpyG3LSw_w
&fb_source=message

Fearon, J. D. (1999, Nov 3). What Is Identity (As We Now Use the
Word)? *Stanford University.* http://www.stanford.edu/~jfea
ron/papers/iden1v2.pdf

Feldman, S. (2019, Oct 30). A visual representation of America's
digital literacy. *Weforum.* https://www.weforum.org/agenda/
2019/10/americans-get-a-failing-grade-for-digital-literacy

Ferguson, R., Gutberg, J., Schattke, K., Paulin, M., & Jost, N.
(2015). Self-determination theory, social media, and
charitable cau ses: An in-depth analysis of autonomous
motivation. *Euro- pe an Journal of Social Psychology, 45*(3):
298–307. DOI: 10.100 2/ejsp.2038.
https://psycnet.apa.org/record /2015-048 57-001

Ferrada Cubillos, M. (2013, Abr). Términos de uso frecuente en la
Web Social, Glosario [Terms of frequent use on the Social
Web, Glossary]. *Serie Bibliotecología y Gestión de
Información,* 81. Santiago, Chile, Universidad Tecnológica
Metropolitana.

http://eprints.rclis.org/19182/1/Serie%20N%C2%B08
1%20Mariela%20Ferrada.pdf

Fernández Delgado, J. (2018, May). Del jeroglífico al emoticono:
cinco mil años de historia de la escritura [From hieroglyphics
to emoticon: five thousand years of writing history]. *Letra*,
Revista digital de la Asociación de Profesores de Español
Francisco de Quevedo de Madrid, Spain, 15(8): 1-78. http://
www.letra15.es/repositorio/L15-08/ L15-08-41-Javier.Fernan
dez.Delgado-Del-jeroglifico.al.emoticono.Cinco.mil.anos.de.
historia.de.la.escritura.pdf

Fernández Moncada, K. (2019). *Manifestaciones Identitarias a tra
vés de la Red Social Facebook* [Identity Demonstrations
through the Facebook Social Network]. Thesis, Santiago de
Cali, Colombia. Universidad de San Buenaventura. http://4
5.5.172.45/b itstream/10819/6804/1/Manifestaciones_Iden
titarias_Facebook_Fernandez_2018%20.pdf

Ferreiro, H. (2012). La teoría hegeliana de la abstracción [The Hege
lian Theory of Abstraction]. *Apuntes filosóficos,* 21(41), pp.
76-88. https://philpapers.org/rec/FE RLAE-2

Fishwick, C. (2016, Mar 17). Narcissist – Vanity, Social Media, and
The Human Condition. *The Guardian.* https://www.theguardi
an.com/world/2016/mar/17/i-narcissist-vanity-social-media-
and-the-human-condition

Floridi, L. (2019, Summer). Semantic Conceptions of Information.
The Stanford Encyclopedia of Philosophy. Edward N. Zalta,
ed. [Web Page]. https://plato.stanford.edu/archives/sum20
19/entries/information-semantic.

Forzani, E. y Leu, D. J. (2012). Necesidad de tecnologías digitales
en las aulas de primaria. [Need for digital technologies in pri
mary school classrooms.]. *The Educational Forum*, 76: 421–

424.

Foucault, M. (2018).*Parrhesia: Berani Berkata Benar*. Marjin Kiri.

Foucault, M. (2001). Fearless Speech. Edited by Josepb Pearson *Semiotext(e)*. https://monoskop.org/images/b/ba/Foucault_ Michel_Fearless_Speech.pdf

Francis, N. & Hoefel, F. (2018, Nov 12). Características de la Gene ración Z y sus implicaciones para las empresas. ['True Gen': Generation Z and its implications for companies]. *McKinsey*. https: //www.mckinsey.com/industries/consumer-packaged- goods/our-insights/true-gen-generation-z-and-its- implications-for-companies

Freire, P. (2005). *Pedagogía del oprimido* [Pedagogy of the oppress ed], 55 ed. Madrid: Siglo XXI.

Frolov, V.V., Adams, G. S., Ahmidouch, G., Armstrong, C. S., Assa magan, K., Avery S. & Davidson, R. M. (1999): Electroprodu ction of the Δ (1232) resonance at high momentum transfer. *Physical Review Letters*, 82(1): 45.

Fuchs, C. (2014). *Social Media: A Critical Introduction*. Lon dres, UK: Sage.

Gabriel (2017, Jan 5). El Emoji Como Signo de Lenguaje en la Ge neración Millennial [The Emoji As a Sign of Language in the Millennial Generation]. *Medium* [Web Page]. https://medium. com/@discontentisimo/el-emoji-como-signo-de-lenguaje-en- la-generaci%C3%B3n-millennial-6876c641cdf1

Galera, J. C. (2017) Instagram, la red social que más rápido crece. Expansión. [Web Page]. https://www.expansion.com/econo mia-digital/innovacion/2017/05/17/591b23cde2704e917f8b4 67c.html

Gallagher, K. (2017, August 4). The social media demographics report: Differences in age, gender and income at the top platforms. *Business Insider.* https://www.businessinsider.com/ the-social-media-demographics-report-2017-8

Gamero, R. (2009, Jun). La construcción de la identidad digital. [The Construction of the Digital Identity]. *EnterIE*, 131. http://www.enter.ie.edu/enter/mybox/cms/11569.pdf

García, O., Flores, N. & Spotti, M., Eds. (2017). *Oxford Handbook of Language and Society.* Oxford: UK, Oxford University Press.

García Canclini, N. (1993). El consumo cultural y su estudio en México: una propuesta teórica. [Cultural consumption and its study in Mexico: a theoretical proposal]. In N. García Canclini (coord.), El consumo cultural en México, pp. 15-42, Conaculta, México, 1993.

Gawne, L., & McCulloch, G. (2019). Emoji as digital gestores. *Language @internet*, *17*(2). https://www.languageatinternet.org/ articles/2019/gawne

Gawne, L. & McCulloch, G. (2018). Emoji Grammar as Beat Gestures. In: S. Wijeratne, E. et al., eds. (2018, Jun 25). *Proceedings of the 1st International Workshop on Emoji Understanding and Applications in Social Media* (Emoji 2018). http://knoe sis.org/resources/Emoji2018/Emoji2018_Papers /Paper13_Emo ji2018.pdf

Gawne, L. & McCulloch, G. (2019). Emoji as digital gestures. *Language@Internet*, 17, article 2. https://www.languageatin ternet.org/articles/2019/gawne

Gee, J. P. (2012). Lo viejo y lo nuevo en las nuevas

alfabetizaciones digitales. [The old and the new in the new digital literacies]. *The Educational Forum*, 76: 418-420.

González-Munné, P. (2014) *Máquina de Quimeras*. [Quimera Machine]. Editorial Letra Viva. Coral Gables, FL.

Grady, J. E., T. Oakley y S. Coulson. (1999). Blending and metaphor. in R. W. Gibbs y G. J. Steen (eds). *Metaphor in cognitive linguistics*. Amsterdam, John Benjamins.

Generación Anáhuac. (2019, Feb 20). La influencia de la tecnologia en nuestra vida cotidiana. [The influence of technology on our daily lives]. https://www.anahuac.mx/generacion-ana huac/la-influencia-de-la-tecnologia-en-nuestra-vida-cotidiana

Giannakopoulou, V. (2019, Dec). Introduction: Intersemiotic Translation as Adaptation: In Memoriam of Laurence Raw Adaptation, 12(3), 199–205. DOI: 10.1093/adaptation/apz023. https: //academic.oup.com/adaptation/article-abstract/12/3/199/56 45646?redirectedFrom= fulltext

Gilster, P. (1997). *Digital Literacy*. New York, NY: John Wiley & Son s, Inc.

Giones Valls, A. & Serrat i Brustenga, M. (2010, June). La gestión de la identidad digital: una nueva habilidad informacional y di gital. [Digital identity management: a new informational and digital skill]. *BiD*: Textos Universitaris De Biblioteconomia I Documentació, 24. https://bid.ub.edu/24/giones2.htm. DOI: dx.doi.org/10.1344/105.000001545.

Goldman, E. (2018, Jun, 4). Emojis and the Law. *Washington Law Review*, 93(1227):1-68. Santa Clara Univ. Legal Studies Research Paper, No. 2018-06. https://papers.ss rn.com/sol3/ papers.cfm?abstract_id=3133412

Gómez, I. (2014). Del meme al imeme, trascendiendo la dimensión lúdica. *Entretextos,* 15, pp. 1-9.

González García, A. (2012). *Prácticas de Socialización de Los Na tivos Digitales: Capital Social en Las Redes Virtuales* [Digital Native Socialization Practices: Social Capital in The Virtual Networks]. Master Thesis. Tijuana, B. C., México: El Colegio de la Frontera Norte. https://colef.repositorioinstitucional.mx/ jspui/bitstream/1014/33/1/TESIS %20-%20Gonza%CC%81 lez%20Garci%CC%81a%20Alejandro.pdf

Greene, J. O. & Burleson, B. R. (2003) *Handbook of Communica tion and Social Interaction Skills*. Mahwah, New Jersey: Lawrence Erlbaum Associates, Inc., Publishers. https://ismailsun ny.files.wordpress.com/2017/07/handbook-of-communication-and-social-interaction-skills.pdf

Greimas, A. J., & Courtés, J. (1982). *Semiotics and language: An analytical dictionary*. Bloomington, IN: Indiana Univ. Press.

Gries, S. T. & Berez, A. L. (2017). Linguistic Annotation in/for Cor pus Linguistics. DOI: 10.1007/978-94-024-0881-2_15. In Ide, Nancy & Pustejovsky, James (eds). *Handbook of Linguistic Annotation,* Berlin, Germany: Springer. pp 379-409. https:// scholarspace.manoa.hawaii.edu/bitstream/10125/506 93/1/ GriesBerez_2017_LinguisticAnnotationInForCorpusLin guistics.pdf

Gumperz, J. J. & Bennet, A. (1981). *Lenguaje y cultura*. Barcelona, Spain: Editorial Anagrama.

Gumperz, J. J., ed. (1997). *Language and Social Identity. Studies in International Sociolinguistics, 2*. Cambridge, UK: Cambridge University Press.

Gumperz, J. J. & Cook-Gumperz, J. (1997). Introduction: Language and the communication of social identity. In Gumperz, John J., Drew, Paul & Goodwin, Marjorie H., eds. (1997). *Langua ge and Social Identity. Studies in International Sociolinguistics, 2.*, Chapter 1, pp. 1-21.

Gutiérrez Martín, A. (2003). Alfabetización digital. Algo más que bo tones y teclas. [Digital literacy. More than just buttons and ke ys]. Barcelona: Gedisa

Haight, M., Quan-Haase, A., & Corbett, B. A. (2014). Revisiting the digital divide in Canada: the impact of demographic factors on access to the internet, level of online activity, and social networking site usage. *Information, Communication & Society*, 17(4): 503-519. Doi:10.1080/1369118X.2014.891633.

Harris, Z. S. (1981). Discourse Analysis. In: Hiż H. (eds). *Papers on Syntax. Synthese Language Library* (Text and Studies in Linguistics and Philosophy), vol 14. Springer, Dordrecht. https ://doi.org/10.1007/978-94-009-8467-7_7

Harris, Z. S. & Hiż, H., ed. (1981). *Papers on Syntax. Synthese Lan guage Library* (Text and Studies in Linguistics and Philosophy). Springer, Dordrecht.

Hassan, A. (2019). El discurso xenófobo en el ámbito político y su impacto social. [Xenophobic discourse in the political sphe re and its social impact]. http://www.scielo.org.co

Hauthal, E., Burghardt, D, & Dunkel, A. (2019, Feb 28). Analyzing and Visualizing Emotional Reactions Expressed by Emojis in Location-Based Social Media. *ISPRS Int. J. Geo-Inf.* 8(113), 1-21. https://www.mdpi.com/2220-9964/8/3/113

Haya, P. (2020, Feb). Somos animales sociales, y esto lo podemos medir. Evento AERCOImas. Asociación para el Desarrollo de la Ingeniería del Conocimiento Madrid. https://www.iic. uam.es/digital/animales-sociales/

Hegel, G. W. F. (1830) Logic. Being Part One of the *Encyclopaedia of The Philosophical Sciences*. Translated by William Wallace with a Foreword by Andy Blunden, 2nd Ed. Pacifica, CA: Marxists Internet Archive, 2013. https://www.marxists.org/ admin/books/hegels-logic/Hegels-Logic.pdf

Helsper, E. & Enyon, R. (2009). Nativos digitales: ¿dónde está la evidencia? [Digital natives: where is the evidence?]. Br Educ Res J. 36: 503–520

Hennig-Thurau, T., Gwinner, K. P., Walsh, G. & Gremler, D. D. (2004): Electronic word-of-mouth via consumer-opinion platforms: What motivates consumers to articulate themselves on the Internet? *Journal of Interactive Marketing*, 18(1): 38-52.

Herrero Gutiérrez, F. J., Trenta, M., Rodríguez Breijo, V., Toledano Buendía, S., Hernández Rodríguez, C. E. & Ardèvol Abreu, A. I., Eds. (2018, Dec). *Comunicación y música: mensajes, manifestaciones y negocios* [Communica- tion and music: messages, manifestations and business]. 2nd ed. Cuadernos Artesanos de Comunicación, CAC 155. 2ª edición ampliada. Doi: 10.418 5/cac155. http://www.revistalatinacs.org/18SLC S/2018_libro2/002_Esparza.pdf

Herring, S. C. (2008). Language and the Internet. In Donsbach, Wol fang (ed.), *International Encyclopedia of Communication*, pp. 2640–2645. Doi: 10.1002/9781405186407.wbiecl0 05

Herring, S. (2013, Jan). Discourse in Web 2.0: Familiar, reconfigu red and emergent. In Tannen, Deborah & Tester, Anna M.

(Eds.), *Georgetown Univ. Round Table on Languages and Linguistics 2011: Discourse 2.0: Language and new media.* https://www.researchgate.net/publication/283612160_Discourse_in_web_20_Familiar_reconfigured_and_emergent

Herring, S. C. (1996a). Introduction. En S. C. Herring (Ed.), Computer-Mediated Communication: Linguistic, Social and Cross-Cultural Perspectives (pp. 1-10). Amsterdam: John Benjamins. doi:10.1075/pbns.39

Herring, S. C. (1996b). Linguistic and Critical Analysis of Computer-Mediated Communication: Some Ethical and Scholarly Considerations. The Information Society, 12(2), 153-168. Doi:10.1080/911232343

Herring, S. C. (1996c). Two variants of an electronic message schema. In S. C. Herring (Ed.), Computer-Mediated Communication. Linguistic, Social and Cross-Cultural Perspectives (pp. 81-106). Amsterdam: John Benjamins. doi:10.1075/pbns.39

Herring, S. C. (2001). Computer-mediated discourse. En D. Schriffin, D. Tannen, & H. Hamilton (Eds.), The Handbook of Discourse Analysis (pp. 612-634). Cornwall: Blackwell.

Herring, S. C. (2004a). Computer-Mediated Communication and Woman's Place. In M. Bucholtz (Ed.), Language and Woman's Place: Text and Commentaries (pp. 216-222). Nueva York: Oxford University Press.

Herring, S. C. (2004b). Computer-Mediated Discourse Analysis: An Approach to Researching Online Behavior. En S. A. Barab, R. Kling, & J. H. Gray (Eds.), *Designing for Virtual Communities in the Service of Learning* (pp. 338-376). Nueva York: Cambridge University Press.

Herring, S. C. (2006). Interactional Coherence in CMC. *Journal of Computer-Mediated Communication*, 4(4). Doi:10.1111/j.10 83-6101.1999.tb00106.x

Herring, S. C. (2007). A Faceted Classification Scheme for Com puter-Mediated Discourse. Language@Internet, 1-37. http:// www.languageatinternet.org/articles/2007/761

Herring, S. C. (2010). Computer-Mediated Conversation: Introduc tion and Overview. Language@Internet, 7. http://www.lan guageatinternet.org/articles/2010/2801

Herring, S. C. (2011). Commentary: Contextualizing Digital Discour se. In C. Thurlow & K. Mroczek (Eds.), Digital Discourse: Language in the new media (pp. 340-347). Nueva York: Oxford University Press.

Herring, S. C. (2013). Discourse in Web 2.0: Familiar, Reconfigured, and Emergent. In D. Tannen & A. M. Trester (Eds.), Discour se 2.0. Language and New Media (pp. 1-25). Washington: Georgetown University Press.

Herring, S. C. (2015a). New frontiers in interactive multimodal com munication. En A. Georgakopoulou & T. Spilloti (Eds.), The Routledge handbook of language and digital communication (pp. 398-402). Londres: Routledge.

Herring, S. C. (2015b). The co-evolution of computer-mediated dis course analysis an computer-mediated communication. Ponencia presentada en la 1st International Conference Approaches to Digital Discourse Analysis (ADDA). Valencia, 18-20 de noviembre de 2015.

Herring, S. C., & Stoerger, S. (2014). Gender and (A)nonymity in Computer-Mediated Communication. En S. Ehrlich, M.

Meyerhoff, & J. Holmes (Eds.), The Handbook of Language, Gen der, and Sexuality (2.a ed., pp. 567–586). Chichester: John Wiley & sons.

Herring, S. C., & Zelenkauskaite, A. (2009). Symbolic capital in a virtual heterosexual market. Abbreviation and insertion in Italian iTV SMS. Written Communication, 26(1), 5-31.

Heuer, R. J. (1999). *Psychology of Intelligence Analysis.* Center for the Study of Intelligence. Central Intelligence Agency Foreword by Douglas MacEachin, Introduction by Jack Davis. https://www.cia.gov/library/center-for-the-study-of-intelligen ce/csi-publications/books-and-monographs/psychology-of-intelligence-analysis/PsychofIntel New.pdf

Hicks, S. D. (2011). Tecnología en el aula de hoy: ¿Eres un maes tro experto en tecnología? [Technology in Today's Classroom: Are You a Tech-Savvy Teacher?]. *The Clearing Hou se*, 84 (5): 188-191.

Hinz, O., Skiera, B., Barrot, C. & Becker, J. U. (2011). Seeding strat egies for viral marketing: An empirical comparison. *Journal of Marketing*, 75(6): 55-71.

Hockly, N. (2011). Technology for the language teacher Digital Liter acies. *ELT Journal*. 66(1): 108-112. Doi: 10.1093/elt/ccr077. https://www.researchgate.net/publica tion/275133288_Digital_literacies

Høigilt, J. & Mejdell, G., Eds. (2016). *The Politics of Written Langua ge in the Arab World: Writing Change.* Boston, MA: Brill Publishers. http://www.jstor. org/stable/10.1163/j.ctt1w76vkk.17

Holmes, J. & Wilson, N. (2017, Feb 10). *An Introduction to Sociolin*

guistics, 5th Ed. London, UK: Routledge Publishers. Doi: 10.
  4324/9781315728438. http://home.lu.
  lv/~pva/Sociolingvistika/1006648_82038_wardhaugh_r_an_i
  ntroduction_to_sociolinguistics.pdf

Holton, D. (2010). Jamie McKenzie, Nativismo digital, delirios digita
  les y privación digital. EdTechDev, De Ahora en Adelante:
  La Revista de Tecnología Educativa, 17(2).

Hutchinson, A. (2017, Feb 18). Facebook Reactions a Year on –
  How are Reactions Being Used and What Does That Tell
  Us? Social Media Today [Web Page]. https ://www.social
  mediatoday.com/social-networks/facebook-reactions-year-
  how-are-reaction s-being-used-and-what-does-tell-us

Hymes, D., 2013. Foundations in sociolinguistics: Ethnographic
  approach. Routledge. DOI: https://doi.org/10.4324/978131
  5888835

Icaza-Álvarez, D. O., Campoverde-Jiménez, G. E., Verdugo-Orma-
  za, D. E. & Arias-Reyes, P. D. (2019, Feb). El analfabetismo
  tecnológico o digital Technological or digital illiteracy.
  Analfabetismo tecnológico ou digital. Polo del Conocimiento,
  30 (4)2: 1-60 DOI: 10.23857/pc.v4i2.922.
  https://dialnet.unirioja .es/descarga/articulo/7164297.pdf

Ide, N. & Pustejovsky, J., eds. (2017). Handbook of Linguistic An
  notation, Berlin, Germany: Springer Science+Business
  Media Dordrecht.

Islas, O. (2008). La Sociedad de la Ubicuidad, los Prosumidores y
  un Modelo de Comunicación para Comprender la
  Complejidad de las Comunicaciones Digitales. [The Ubiquity
  Society, Prosumers, and a Communication Model for
  Understanding the Complexity of Digital Communications].
  http://revista.pu

balaic.org/index.php/alaic/article/download/45/44

Islas-Carmona, J. O. (2008, Jun). El prosumidor. El actor comunicati vo de la sociedad de la ubicuidad. [The communicative actor of the society of ubiquity]. *Palabra Clave*, 11(1). http://www. scielo.org.co/pdf/pacla/v11n1/v11n01a03.pdf

Iyengar, S., Lelkes, Y., Levendusky, M., Malhotra, N. & Westwood, S. J. (2019). The Origins and Consequences of Affective Polarization in the United States. *Annual Review of Political Science,* 22(1): 129-146. https://www.dartmouth.edu/~sean jwestwood/papers/ARPS.pdf

Jakobson, R. (1960). Linguistics and Poetics. in T. Sebeok, ed., *Style in Language*, Cambridge, MA: M.I.T. Press. pp. 350-377.

Jakobson, R. (1959). On linguistic aspects of translation. In Lawrence Venuti & Mona Baker (Eds.) *The Translation Studies Reader*. Routledge, a Taylor & Francis Group. pp. 113-118. https://translationjournal.net/images/e-Books/PDF_Files/ The% 20 Translation%20Studies%20 Reader.pdf

Jenkins, H. (2006). *Convergence culture: culture of media conver gence*. New York, NY: New York University Press. https:// www.hse.ru/data/2016/03/15/1127638366/Henry%20Jenkins %20Convergence%20culture%20where%20old%20 and%20new%20media%20collide%20%202006.pdf

Jenkins, H. (2008). *Convergence culture: la cultura de la convergen cia de los medios de comunicación* [Convergence culture: culture of media convergence]. Barcelona, Spain: Paidós Ibé rica. https://stbngtrrz.files.wordpress.com/2012/10/jenkins-henry-convergence-culture.pdf

Jha, C. K., & Kodila-Tedika, O. (2020). Does social media promote democracy? Some empirical evidence. *Journal of Policy Modeling*, 42(2): 271-290.

Jiménez Redondo, M. (2012). Parresía y diferencia ética: consideraciones sobre el último Foucault. [Parresia and ethical difference: considerations about the last Focalult]. in: Bermúdez, J. A., Ed. (2012). *Michael Foucault, un pensador poliédrico*. PUV: 121-142. https://roderic.uv.es/handle/10550/52666

Joiner, R, Gavin, J, Brosnan, M, Cromby, J, Gregory, H, Guiller, J, Maras, P & Moon, A. (2013). Comparando el uso de Internet de nativos digitales de primera y segunda generación, ansiedad por Internet y identificación de Internet. *Cyberpsychology, Behavior, and Social Networking*, 16(7): 549-552.

Jones, R. H., Chik, A., & Hafner, C. A. (2015). Introduction: Discourse analysis and digital practices. In R. H. Jones, A. Chik, & C. A. Hafner, Eds. *Discourse analysis and digital practices: Doing discourse analysis in the digital age,* pp. 1-17. London: Rout ledge

Jones, C., Ramanau, R., Cross, SJ y Healing, G. (2010). Net generation o nativos digitales: ¿Existe una nueva generación distinta que ingresa a la universidad? Informática y educación. Vol 54 (3) pp722-732.

Jones, C. & Shao, B. (2011). *La generación neta y los nativos digitales: implicaciones para la educación superior*. Academia de Educación Superior, York.

Jones, C. & Shao, B. (2010, Mar 4). Tecnología y sociedad: ¿Es realmente útil hablar de una nueva generación de nativos digitales que han crecido con Internet? [Is it really useful to talk about a new generation of digital natives who have grown up with the Internet?]. *The Economist*.

Jost, J. T. & Sidanius, J. (Eds.). (2004). *Key readings in social psychology. Political psychology.* Psychology Press. DOI: 10. 4324/9780203505984. https://www.taylorfrancis.com/bo oks/e/97 80203505984

Jovanovic, D. & Van Leeuwen, T. (2018). Multimodal dialogue on social media. *Social Semiotics, 28*(5), 683–699. DOI:10.10 80/10350330.2018.150473. https://www.tandfonline.com/doi / abs/10.1080/10350330.2018.1504732

Kaakinen, M., Sirola, A., Savolainen, I., & Oksanen, A. (2018). Sha red identity and shared informa tion in social media: development and validation of the identity bubble reinforcement sca- le. *Media Psychology, 23*(1), 25-51. DOI: 10.1080/152 13269 .2018.1544910. https://www. researchgate.net/public cation/3 29058285_Shared_identity_and_shared_informa tion_in_social_media_development_and_validation_of_the_i dentity_bubble_reinforcement_scale

Kaplan, A. M. & Haenlein, M. (2010). Users of the world, unite! The challenges and opportunities of social media. *Business Horizons*, 53(1): 59-68.

Kaplún, M. (1985). El Comunicador Popular. Ecuador. Editorial Be lén.

Karam, T. (2005). Una introducción al estudio del discurso y al aná lisis del discurso [An Introduction to the study of discourse and the analysis of speech]. *Global Media Journal Edición Iberoamericana*, 2(3), pp.34-50. http://gmje.mty.itesm.mx/ articu los 3/articulo_5.html

Kavanaugh, A., Carroll, J.M., Rosson, M.D., Zin, T.T. & Reese, D.D.

(2005), Community Networks: Where Offline Communities Meet Online. *Journal of Computer-Mediated Communication*, 10(4). http://jcmc.indiana.edu/vol10/issue4/kavanaugh.html

Keane, J. (2011, May 18). Democracy in the age of Google, Face book and WikiLeaks. Article, University of Melbourne. Public lecture delivered in the Council of Europe Democracy Deba te Series, Strasbourg, Tuesday July 5th, 2011. https://www. coe.int/t/ dgap/forum-democracy/Activities/Democracy%20 Debates/Keane_speech.pdf

Kelly, K. (1994, Oct 1). *Out of Control: The New Biology of Machi nes, Social Systems, and the Economic World*. La Vergne, Tennessee: Ingram Content Group. https: //kk.org/mt-files /books-mt/ooc-mf.pdf

Kelly, K. (1999, Oct 1). *New Rules for the New Economy: 10 Radi cal Strategies for a Connected World*. New York, NY: Penguin and Random House Publishers. https://kk.org/mt-files/ books-mt/KevinKelly-NewRules-withads.pdf

Kendall, L. (2002). *Hanging out in the virtual pub: Masculinities and relationships online*. Berkeley, CA: University of California Press.

Kennedy, G., Judd, T. & Dalgarno, B. (2010). Más allá de los nati vos y los inmigrantes: Explorando los tipos de estudiantes de la generación de la red. [Beyond the Natives and Immigrants: Exploring the Types of Students of the Network Generation]. *Journal of Computer Assisted Learning*, 26(5): 332-343.

Kemp, S. (2020, January 30). Digital 2020: 3.8 billion people use so-cial media. *WeAreSocial*. https://wearesocial.com/blog/2020/ 01/digital-2020-3-8-billion-people-use-social-media#:~:text= Our%20new%20Digital%202020%20reports,people%20all%

20over%20the%20 world

Kirda, E. & Kruegel, C. (2006). Protecting users against phishing at
tacks. *The Computer Journal*, 49(5). http://www.cs.ucsb.edu
/~chris/research/doc/cj06_phish.pdf

Kostadinovska-Stojchevska, B. & Shalevska, E. (2018, Nov). Inter
net Memes and their Socio-Linguistic Features. *European
Journal of Literature, Language and Linguistics Studies*,
https://oapub.org/lit/index.php/EJLLL/article/view/73

Krishen, A. S, Berezan, O., Agarwal, S. & Kachroo, P. (2016, Nov).
The generation of virtual needs: Recipes for satisfaction in
social media networking. *Journal of Business Research*, 69
(11): 5248-5254. http://anjala.faculty.unlv.edu/Krishen
Berezan_JBR_2016.pdf

Kristensson, P. O. & Vertanen, K. (2014). The Inviscid Text Entry
Rate and its Application as a Grand Goal for Mobile Text
Entry. In Proceedings of the 16th International conference on
Human-computer interaction with mobile devices & services
- *MobileHCI '14*. ACM Press, New York. DOI: http://dx.doi.
org/10.1145/2628363.2628405

Lake, A, (2017). *The State of The World's Children 2017. Children
in a Digital World*. New York, NY: United Nations Children's
Fund, UNICEF. https://www.unicef.org/publictions/files/SO
WC_2017_ ENG_WEB.pdf

Lankshear, C., & Knobel, M. (2008). *Digital Literacies: Concepts, Po
licies, and Practices*. New York: Peter Lang.

Lara, T. (2012). Twitter y sus funciones comunicativas. [Twitter and
its communicative functions]. *Blog Tíscar.com*. http://tiscar.
com/2012/03/11/twitter-y-sus-funciones-comunicativas

Lasswell, H. (1948). The Structure and Function of Communication in Society. In Bryson, L. (ed.). *The Communication of Ideas*. New York: Institute for Religious and Social Studies. http://si pa.jlu.edu.cn/__local/E/39/71/4CE63D3C04A10B5795F010 8EBE6_A7BC17AA_34AAE.pdf

Latif, E. A. (2017). The Oralization of Writing: Argumentation, Pro fanity and Literacy in Cyberspace. In Høigilt, Jacob & Mejdell Gunvor, Eds. (2016). *The Politics of Written Language in the Arab World: Writing Change*, Chapter 12, pp. 290-308. Boston, MA: Brill Pu=-blishers. http://www.jstor.org/stable/10.11 63/j.ctt1w76vkk.17

Lea, M., & Spears, R. (1992). Paralanguage and Social Perception in ComputerMediated Communication. *Journal of Organizational Computing*, 2:3(4): 321-341.

Ledesma Ríos, G. P., Zarate Castillo, N. & Velasco Espinosa, E. (2018, Jul-Dec). Jóvenes en las redes sociales. Caso Facebook [Young people in social networks, case Facebook]. *Revista Mexicana de Orientación Educativa*, 15(35): pp. 1-20. DOI: 10.31206 /rmdo062018. https://www.re searchgate.net /publication/330022612s_Jovenes_en_las_redes_so ciales_ Caso_Facebook

Lei, J. (2009). Nativos digitales como futuros profesores: ¿qué pre paración tecnológica se necesita? [Digital natives as future teachers: what Technological preparation is needed?]. *Journal of Computing in Teacher Education*, Spring. 25 (3): 89.

Levoyer, S. & Escandón Montenegro, P. A. (2018). Información y datos en campañas transmedia [Information and data in transmedia campaigns], In López Golán, M., Campos Freire, F., López López, Paulo C. & Rivas Echeverría, F., Eds., *La comunicación en la nueva sociedad digital* [Communication in the new digital Society], 1st ed., pp. 435-453. https://www. amic.media/media/files/file_352_1557.pdf

Li, Li & Yang, Yue (2018, Dec). Pragmatic functions of emoji in inter netbased communication--a corpus-based study. *Asian-Pa cific Journal of Second and Foreign Language Education*, 3 (16): 1-12. Pragmatic functions of emoji in internet-based communication---a corpus-based study. DOI: 10.1186/s408 62-018-0057-z. https://link.springer.com/ article/10.1186/s4 0862-018-0057-z

Licona, N. (2018, Aug 14). Tecnología y su Aplicación. https://jcyenl m.blogspot.com/2018/12/tecnologia-su-aplicacion-los-equipo s-de_14.html

Light, L. (2017). Perspectives: An Open Invitation to Cultural Anthro Pology. In Nina Brown, Thomas McIlwraith, Laura Tubelle de González. (2017). *Perspectives: An Open Invitation to Cultu ral Anthropology* 2nd E. American Anthropological Association. https://courses.lumenlearning.com/suny-culturalanthro pology/chapter/language

Lichtańska, K. & Cygan, B. (2020). School Skills of Digital Natives in the Context of Functional Illiteracy. *Przegląd Pedagogiczny*, 1, 254–267. DOI 10.34767/PP.2020.01.15. http://yadda.icm. edu.pl/yadda/element/bwmeta1.element.desklight-5b31abfe-7f65-4457-8d26-83caef10cd84

Livingston, J. A. (2005). How valuable is a good reputation? a sam ple selection model of Internet auctions. *The Review of Economics and Stadistics*, vol. 87, p. 453–465.

Livingstone, S., Haddon, L., Görzig, A. & Ólafsson, K. (2011) Risks and safety on the internet: the perspective of European children: full findings and policy implications from the EU Kids Online survey of 9–16-year-olds and their parents in 25 countries. EU Kids Online, Deliverable D4. EU Kids Onli ne Network, London, UK. http://eprints.lse.ac.uk/33731/1/ Risks%20and%20safety%20on%20the%20internet%28Iser o%29.pdf

López Golán, M., Campos Freire, F., López López, Paulo C. & Ri vas Echeverría, F., Eds. (2018). *La comunicación en la nueva sociedad digital* [Communication in the new digital Society]. 1st ed. Published in collaboration by the Pontificia Universidad Católica del Ecuador Sede Ibarra, Universidad Técnica Particular de Loja, Universidade de Santiago de Compostela, Pontificia Universidad Católica del Ecuador y el Con sejo de Publicaciones de la Universidad de Los Andes. https://www.amic.media/ media/files/file_352_1557.pdf

López Poza, S. & Pena Sueiro, N., Eds. (2014). *Humanidades Digi tales: desafíos, logros y perspectivas de futuro* [Digital Huma nities: Challenges, Achievements and future prospects]. SIELAE, Seminario Interdisciplinar para el Estudio de la Literatura Áurea Española. Facultad de Filología. A Coruña, Spain: Universidade da Coruña. https://www.janusdigital.es/ anexo/descargar.htm;jsessionid=38D7D62CDFF3DD1F86 B4EDA5B500C508?id=5

Maingueneau, D. (2017, Jul 4). The heterogeneity of discourse: Ex panding the field of discourse analysis. *Palgrave Communications*, 3, Article number 17058. DOI: 10.1057/palcomms. 2017.58. https://www.nature.com/articles/palcomms201758

Maffesoli, M. (1988). *El tiempo de las tribus. El declive del individua lismo en la sociedad de masas*. Barcelona, Spain: Icaria.

Maffesoli, M. (1996). *The Times of Tribes. The decline of individuali sm in mass society*. New York, NY: Sage Publications.

Mancera Rueda, A. (2011) *¿Cómo se "habla" en los cibermedios? El español coloquial en el periodismo digital.* Bern, Switzerland: Peter Lang AG. DOI: 10.3726/978-3-0351-0297-0.
https://www.academia.edu/1076636/_C%C3%B3mo_se_habla_en_los_cibermedios_El_espa%C3%B1ol_coloquial_en_el_periodismo_digital

Mancera Rueda, A. y Pano Alamán, A. (2014, Nov 4). Las redes so ciales como corpus de estudio para el Análisis del discurso mediado por ordenador [Social media as a Study corpus for Computer Mediated Speech Analysis]. In *Humanidades Digitales: desafíos, logros y perspectivas de futuro*, López Poza, Sagrario & Pena Sueiro, Nieves (eds.), *Janus,* Anexo 1, pp. 305–315.
https://dialnet.unirioja.es/servlet/articulo?codigo= 5181037

Marcelo, C. & Perera, V. H. (2006, Dec). Sequences of Discourse in e-Learning Environments. *Academic Exchange Quarterly*, 10(4), pp. 268-273. https://www.ac ademia.edu/26602128/ Sequences_of_Discourse_in_e-Learning_Environments

Markus, M. L. (1994). Finding a Happy Medium: Explaining the Neg ative Effects of Electronic Communication on Social Life at Work. ACM Transactions. In DOI: ri14.v13i1.716. Año 2015, 13(1). *ICONO14.* La expresión de las emociones en la Comunicación Virtual: *El Ciberhabla*, 206, Information Systems, 12(1): 119–149.

Markman, K. M., & Oshima, S. Pragmatic Play? Some Possible Functions of English Emoticons and Japanese Kaomoji in Computer-Mediated Discourse. Presented at the Association of Internet Researchers Annual Conference 8.0: *Let's Play!* In Vancouver, B.C., Canada. https://doi.org/10.31235/OSF.

IO/QA764. https://osf.io/preprints/socarxiv/qa764/

Marín Pérez, T. (2018, Mar 9). *Lazos. Cuerpo Orgánico En La Cultu ra Digital* [Ties. Organic Body in Digital Culture]. Master Thesis. Foz do Iguaçu, Brazil, *Universidade Federal da Integra ção Latino-Americana*. https://dspace.unila.edu.br/ bitstream/ handle /123456789/3649/disertaci%C3% B3n%20 version% 20final%20con%20fecha.pdf?sequence=1&isAllo wed=y

Martínez, R. (2019, Mar 24). ¿Realmente está Google volviéndonos estúpidos? [Is Google really making us stupid?]. https:// interferencia.cl/articulos/realmente-esta-google-volviendonos-estupidos

Martínez de Sousa, J. (2004). *Ortografía y ortotipografía del espa ñol actual*. [Spelling and spelling of current Spanish]. Gijón, Trea.

Martínez Musiño, C. & Maya Corzo, O. (2004, Aug). 1er Foro Social de Información Documentación y Bibliotecas. Programas de Acción Alternativa desde Latinamérica para la Sociedad del Conocimiento. Buenos Aires, 26-28 Agosto 2004. https://co re.ac.uk/download/pdf/11881435.pdf

Mauss, I. B. & Robinson, M. D. (2009). Measures of emotion: A re view. *Cognition and Emotion*, 23(2), 209-237, DOI: 10.1080/ 02699930802204677. https://www.ncbi.nlm.nih.gov/pmc/articles/PMC2756702/pdf/ nihms134765.pdf https://www.ncbi. nlm.nih.gov/pmc/artcles/PMC2756702/pdf/nihms134765.pdf

McCrindle, M. & Fell, A. (2015, Feb 2). Actualización de la infografía Gen Z y Gen Alpha. [Updating the infographic Gen Z and Gen Alpha]. https://mccrindle.com.au/insights/blogarchive/ gen-z-and-gen-alpha-infographic-update/

McCulloch, G. (2019, Jul 23). *Because Internet: Understanding the New Rules of Language.* New York, NY: Riverhead Books.

McLuhan, M. (1964). *Understanding media. The extensions of man.* New York, NY: Signet Books.

McLuhan, M. (1970). *Counterblast.* London, UK: Pitman Press. https ://monos kop.org/images/d/dc/McLuhan_Marshall_1970_Co unterblast.pdf

McLuhan, M. & Nevitt, B. (1972). Take today: The executive as drop out. New York, NY: Harcourt Brace Jovanovich.

McWhorter, J. (2013, Feb). Txting is kinlling language. JK!!! *TED Talks.* [Web Video]. https://www.ted.com/talks/john_mcwhor ter_txtng_is_killing_language_jk

Mehmet, M., Clarke, R. J., & Kautz, K. (2014). *Social media semantics: analysing meanings in multimodal online conversations.* [Paper presentation]. International Conference on Information Systems, pp. 1-15. New Zealand: University of Auckland. https://ro.uow.edu.au/ buspapers/654/

Meyers, E. M., Erickson, I. & Small, R. V. (2013). Digital literacy and informal learning environments: an introduction. Learning, Media and Technology, 38(4): 355-367. Doi: 10.1080/17439 884.2013.783597

Michalove, P. A., Stefan, G. & Manaster Ramer, A. (1998, Oct). Cur rent Issues in Linguistic Taxonomy. *Annual Review of Anthro pology.* 27, pp. 451-472. Doi: 10.1146/annurev.anthro.27.1. 451. https://www.annualreviews.org/doi/abs/10.1146/annnu rev.anthro.27.1.451

Meissner, P. (2021, Sep 2). These countries rank highest for digital competitiveness. *Webforum*. https://www.weforum.org/agen da/2021/09/countries-rank-highest-digital-competitiveness/

Miranda Villalón, J. A., Olmos Hurtado, A., Ordozgoiti de la Rica, R. & Rodríguez del Pino, D. (2014, Feb). *Publicidad on line. Las claves del éxito en Internet* [Online advertising. The keys to success on the Internet]. 3rd ed. Madrid, Spain: Esic Edito rial. 2010.

Mitcham, C. (2012). La tecnología y el peso de la responsabilidad. *BBVA TF Editores* https://www.bbvaopenmind.com/articulos /la-tecnologia-y-el-peso-de-la-responsabilidad. in *Valores y Ética para el siglo XXI*. https://www.bbvaopenmind.com/wp-content/uploads/2013/02/BBVA-OpenMind-La-tecnolog%C3 %ADa-y-el-peso-de-la-responsabilidad-Carl-Mitcham.pdf.pdf

Moral Toranzo, F. & García Loreto, R. (2003). Un nuevo lenguaje en la red. [A new Language in the Net]. *Comunicar*, 21: 133-136

Morales-López, E. (2011, Jul) Hacia Dónde Va El Análisis del Dis curso [Where Speech Analysis Goes]. *Revista Electrónica de Estudios Filológicos,* 21. [Web Page]. https://www.um.es /tonosdigital/znum21/secciones/estudios-21-discurso.htm

Morera Vidal, F. J. (2017, Sep 22). *Aproximación a la infografía Co mo comunicación efectiva* [Approaching infographic as effective communication]. Doctorate Thesis, Universitat Autòno ma de Barcelona, Spain. https://ddd.uab.cat/pub/tesis/2017/ hdl_10803_457366/fjmv1de1.pdf

Morgan, H. (2014). Uso de proyectos de historias digitales para ayu dar a los estudiantes a mejorar en lectura y escritura. [Using Digital Story Projects to give students better at reading and writing]. *Mejora de la Lectura*, 51 (1): 20-26.

Morozov, E. (2012). *El Desengaño de Internet: Los Mitos de la Liber tad en la Red*. [The Disappointment of the Internet: The Myths of Freedom on the Net]. Imago Mundi. Barcelona: Ediciones Destino./

Morgan, H. (2014). Maximizar el éxito de los estudiantes con un aprendizaje diferenciado. [Maximize student success with a differentiated learning]. *The Clearing House*, 87 (1): 34–38.

Murray, R., Caulier-Grice, J. & Mulgan, G. (2010). *The Open Book of Social Innovation: Ways to Design, Develop and Grow So cial Innovations*. Social Innovator Series: Ways to Design, Develop and Grow Social Innovation. London, UK: The Youn g Foundation & NESTA. https://youngfoundation.org/ wp-con tent/uploads/2012/10/ The-Open-Book-of-Social-Innovation g.pdf

Musgrove, M. (2008, Oct 17). Hablando de la generación digital. *The Washington Post*.

Nath, H. K. (2017, Mar 31). The Information Society. *SIBCOLTEJO*, A Journal of the SCTU, 4: pp. 19-29. https://www.shsu.edu/ eco_ hkn/The%20Information%20Society.pdf

Naughton, J. (1999). *A brief history of the future: the origins of the Internet*. London, UK: Weidenfeld and Nicolson.

Naughton, J. (2016). The evolution of the Internet: from military ex periment to General Purpose Technology. *Journal of Cyber Policy*, 1(1), p. 5-28, DOI: 10.1080/23738871.2016.1157619. https://www.tandfonline.com/doi/pdf/10.1080/23738871.2016 .115 7619?needAccess=true

Newhagen, J. & Rafaeli, S. (1996, Mar 1). Why Communication Re searchers Should Study the Internet: A Dialogue. *Journal of Computer-Mediated Communication*. DOI: 10.1111 /j.1083-

6101.1996.tb00172.x. [Web Page]. https://academic.oup. Com/jcm c/article/1/4/J CMC145/4584318

Nicolacopoulos, T. & Vassilacopoulos, G. (2005). On the Systemic Meaning of Meaningless Utterances: The Place of Language in Hegel's Speculative Philosophy. *Cosmos and History: The Journal of Natural and Social Philosophy.* 1(1): 17-26. https://www.cosmosandhistory.org/index.php/journal/article/view/3/6

Nicolov, N. & Shanahan, J. G. (2011- Jul 17-21). *Proceedings of the 5th International AAAI Conference on Weblogs and Social Media: The Future of the Social Web Workshop* (ICWS M'11), p. 2-5. Menlo Park, CA: AAAI Press. http://www.aaai .org/ Library/ICWSM/icwsm11contents.php

Norman, D. (2013). *The design of everyday things.* Revised and Ex panded Edition. New York, NY: Doubleday Business. https://www.nixdell.com/classes/HCI-and-De sign-Spring-2017/The-Design-of-Everyday-Things-Revised-and-Expanded-Edition.pdf

Obar, J. A. & Wildman, S. S. (2015). Social Media Definition and the Governance Challenge-An Introduction to the Special Issue. Teleco*mmunications Policy*, 39(9): 745-750. Quello Center Working Paper No. 2647377.

Ogden, C. K. & Richards, I. A. (1923). *The Meaning of Meaning. A study of the influence of language upon thought and of the science of symbolism. With supplementary essays by Bronis- ław Malinowski and F. G. Crookshank.* https://archive.org/details/meaningofmeaning00ogde/page/n11/mode/2up?q=so metimes+the+disputants+are+using

Omar, A. & Miah, M. (2013). Digital Evolution of the Written Langua ge. Proceedings of the *Information Systems Educators*

Conference. San Antonio, TX. https://pdfs.semanticscholar.org/6 7d3/1b880223cc6f8ad1d66ca5847dc63b9cfd05.pdf

Ortega Villa, L. M. (2009, Jul-Dec). Consumo De Bienes Culturales: Reflexiones Sobre un Concepto y Tres Categorías para su Análisis. *Culturales*, V(10), ISSN 1870-1191. Universidad Autónoma de Baja California http://www.scielo.org.mx/pdf/ cultural/v5n10/v5n10a2.pdf

Osnos, P. (2013, Feb 26), The Enduring Myth of the 'Free' Internet. *The Atlantic.* https://www.theatlantic.com/technology/archive /2013/02/the-enduring-myth-of-the-free-internet/273515/

O'Toole, P. [Movie Clips]. (1962). Nothing is Written - Lawrence of Arabia (4/8) Movie CLIP (1962) H.D. [YouTube Video]. https ://www.youtube.com/watch?v=_EZCG2Ex8Q0

Ozollo, J. (2015). Marx y el Estado. Determinaciones sociales del pensamiento de Karl Marx. https://bdigital.uncu.edu.ar/objetos_digitales/2687/marx-y-el-estado-final-1.pdf

Padierna Beltrán, Adriana & Esparza Hernández, Carlos Alberto (2018, Dec). La humanización de los discursos digitales [Hu manization of digital discourses]. Doi:10.4185/cil2018-041. In Herrero, Javier & Trenta, Milena, Eds. (2018, Dec) *Comunicación y música: mensajes, manifestaciones y negocios.*

Page, R., Barton, D., Unger, J. & Zappavigna, M. (2014, Jun 27). *Re searching Language and Social Media.* A Student Guide, 1st ed., London, UK: Taylor & Francis Group. Doi: 10.4324/978 1315771786.

Pagel, M. (2017, Jul 24). Q&A: What is human language when did it

evolve and why should we care? *BMC Biology,* 15(64): 1-6.
Doi: 10.1186/s12915-017-0405-3. https://www.ncbi.nlm.nih.
gov/pmc/ articles/PMC5525259/pdf/12915_2017_Article_40
5. pdf

Palazzo, G. (2005). ¿Son corteses los jóvenes en el chat? Estudio
de estrategias de interacción en la conversación virtual. [Are
young people in the chat courteous? I am a student of
interaction strategies in virtual conversation]. *TEXTOS de la
Ci berSociedad,* 5 (2005), [21/09/2013].
http://www.cibersociedad.net

Paradiso, J. A. (2017, Jan). El cerebro sensorial aumentado. Cómo
conectarán los humanos con el internet de las cosas. [The
sensory brain increased. How connect humans to the inter
net of things]. In *El próximo paso La Vida Exponencial.*
https://www.bbvaopenmind.com/wp-content/uploads/2017
/01/BBVA -OpenMind-libro-El-proximo-paso-vida-
exponencial1.pdf

Pauli, M. (2008, Jan 16). Spider-Man loses a wife and upsets comic
Fans. *The Guardian.* https://www.theguardian.com/world/20
08/jan/16/books.filmnews

Paús, M. F. & Macchia, L. (2014). Marketing Viral en medios socia
les: ¿Qué contenido es más contagioso y por qué? [Viral
Social Media Marketing: What content is most contagious
and why?]. *Ciencias Administrativas,* 4.

Mademova, S., Pawlowski, E. & Hudson, L. (2018, May). A Description of U.S. Adults Who Are Not Digitally Literate. *Stats in
Brief.* IES, Institute of Education Sciences. https://nces.ed.
gov/pubs2018/2018161.pdf

Paz, O. (1972) *El arco y la lira* [The Bow and the Lyre]. Ciudad de
Mexico, Mexico: Fondo de Cultura Económica. http://www.ec

frasis.org/wp-content/uploads/2014/ 06/Octavio-Paz-El-arco-y-la-lira.pdf

Pêcheux, M. (1983). Lecture et mémoire: projet de recherche. [Rea ding and dissertation: research project. In: L´inquietude du discours. Paris: des Cendres, p.285-293.

Peck, A. (2015, Summer). Tall, Dark, and Loathsome: The Emergen ce of a Legend Cycle in the Digital Age. *The Journal of Ame rican Folklore,*128(509), pp. 333-348. Doi: 10.5406/jamerfolk .128.509.0333. https://www.jstor.org/stable/10.5406/jamerfol k.128.509.0333

People. (2016, Aug 14). Berkman Klein Center. *Cyber.law*. Harvard.

Perez-Salazar, G., Aguilar, A. & Castellanos, V., eds. (2013, Jan). *La producción del conocimiento en las ciencias de la comunicación y su incidencia social*. [The production of knowled ge in the communication sciences and its social impact]. DOI: 10.13140/RG.2.1.4816.3924. https://www.researchga te.net/publication/289988925_La_produccion_del_conocimie nto_en_las_ciencias_de_la_comunicacion_y_su_inciden cia_social

Pérez Salazar, G., Aguilar Edwards, A. & Guillermo Archilla, M. E. (2014, May-Ago). El meme en internet: Usos sociales, reinterpretación y significados, a partir de Harlem Shake. [The meme on the Internet: Social uses, reinterpretation and mea nings, starting with Harlem Shake]. *Argumentos*, 27(75): 79-100. http://www.scie lo.org.mx/scielo.php?script=sci_arttext &pid=S0187-57952014000200005&lng=es&nrm =iso. OR http://www.scielo.org.mx/pdf/argu/v27n75/v27n75a5.pdf

Pérez Tornero, J. M. (2012, Jan 1). Pensamiento crítico en la edu cación y la comunicación [Critical thinking in education and Communication]. *Servicio Audiovisual UNIA.* Conference in then la inauguration of Master classes for Comunication and Audiovisual Education, Huelva, Spain. https://vimeo.com/11 2471180

Perera, C., Zaslavsky, A. B., Christen, P. & Georgakopoulos, D. (2014). Context Aware Computing for The Internet of Things: A Survey. *IEEE Communications Sur- veys & Tutorials*, 16, 414-454. DOI: 10.1109/SURV.2013.042313.00197. https:// arxiv.org/pdf/1305.0982.pdf

Perkel, D. (2006). Copy and paste literacy: literacy practices in the production of a MySpace profile. *Informal Learning and Digital.* http://people.ischool.berkeley.edu/~dperkel/media/dperkel_lit eracymyspace.pdf

Pinker, S. (Julio, 2005). What our language habits reveal [Archivo de video]. TEDGlobal. https://www.ted.com/talks/steven_pinker_on_language_and_ thought#t-47024

Poell, T. & Van Dijck, J. (2015, Jun 30). Social Media and Activist Communication. https://papers.ssrn.com/sol3/papers.cfm? abstract_id=2624911&download=yes. In Chris Atton (2015). *The Routledge Companion to Alternative and Community Media*, 1st ed., pp. 527-537. London, UK: Routledge.

Pohl, Henning, Domin, Christian & Rohs, Michael (2017, Mar). Be yond just text: Semantic emoji similarity modeling to support expressive communication □ □ □. Association for Computing Machinery, ACM. *Transactions on Computer-Human Interaction*, 24(1), Article 6-41. DOI: 10.1145/3039685. http://www.henningpohl.net/papers/Pohl2017TOCHI.pdf

Porat, M. U. & Rubin, M. R. (1977). *The Information Economy: Natio nal Income, Workforce, and Input-Output Accounts*, 9 volu mes. Office of Telecommunications Special Publication 77-12. Washington D.C. US Department of Commerce. https://fi les.eric.ed.gov/fulltext/ED142212.pdf

Postman, N. (1992). *Tecnópolis. La rendición de la cultura a la tec nología* [Technopolis. The surrender of culture to technolo gy]. Barcelona, Spain: Galaxia Gutenberg.

Postman, N. (1993, Apr). Technopolis. *The surrender of culture to technology*. New York, NY: First Vintage Books Edition. https://www.collier.sts.vt.edu/1504/pdfs/technopoly-neil-postman.pdf

Postman, N. (1986). *Amusing Ourselves to Death*. Penguin Books. https://quote.ucsd.edu/childhood/files/2013/05/postman-amu sing.pdf

Postmes, C., Spears, T R. & Lea, M. (2000). The Formation of Group Norms in Computer-Mediated Communication. *Human Communication Research*, 26(3): 341-371. Doi: 10.11 11/j.1468-2958.2000.tb00761.x

Preece, S. (Ed.). *The Routledge Handbook of Language and Identi ty*. Routledge.

Prensky, M. (2012). *Brain gain: Technology and the quest for digital Wisdom.* Routledge.

Prensky, M. (2012). New issues, new answers: Trivial or powerful? let's be clear on exactly how we are using technology in education. *Educational Technology*, 52(4): 64.

Prensky, M. (2009). H. sapiens digital: From digital immigrants and

digital natives to digital wisdom. *Innovate*, 5(3). http://www.
innovateonline.info

Prensky, M. (2007). How to teach with technology: Keeping both
teachers and students comfortable in an era of exponential
change. In *Emerging Technologies for Learning*, Vol. 2.

Prenksy, M. (2001a). Digital Natives, Digital Immigrants. In *Horizon*,
9(5).

Prenksy, M. (2001b). Digital Natives, Digital Immigrants, Part II. Do
they really think differently? On *Horizon*, 9(6).

Prensky, M. (2001, Sep). Nativos Digitales, Inmigrantes Digitales
Parte 1. [Digital Natives, Digital Immigrants Part 1]. *El
Horizonte*, 9 (5): 1–6. Doi: 10.1108/10748120110424816 .

Protalinski, E. (2016, Jan 27). Over half of Facebook users access
the service only on mobile. *VentureBeat*. https://venturebeat
.com/2016/01/27/over-half-of-facebook-users-access-the-ser
vice-only-on-mobile/

Psico. (2017, Mar 3). El ego y las redes sociales. [The Ego and the
Social Networks]. https://www.psico.mx/articulos/el-ego-y-
las-redes-sociales

Rainie, L. & Wellman, B. (2012). *Networked: The New Social Operat
ing System*. Cambridge, MA: MIT Press. http://www.jstor.
org/stable/j.ctt5vjq62

Quảng Cáo, Nội Dung. (n.d.). Nativo digital. https://hmong.es/wiki/di
gital_native

Ramos, G. & Schleicher, A. (2018). Preparing our Youth for an Inclu
sive and Sustainable World. *The OECD PISA Global Compe
tence Framework*. https://www.oecd.org/education/Global-

competency-for-an-inclusive-world.pdf

Ramonet, I., Assange, J., Chomsky, N., & Sacristán, M. (2016). *El imperio de la vigilancia*. [The empire of surveillance]. Madrid: Clave intelectual. https://www.eldiplo.org/wp-content/uploads/2018/files/7114/6040/1796/INTRODUCCION.pdf

Rendueles, C. (2013). *Sociofobia*. Madrid, Capitán Swing.

Reyes Jofré, D. (2018). Gamificación de espacios virtuales de apren dizaje [Gamification of virtual learning spaces]. *Extos: Estudios De Humanidades y Ciencias Sociales*, (41). http://revistas.umce.cl/index.php/con textos/article/view/1390

Reyes Pérez, A., Rosso, P. & Buscaldi, D. (2012, July). From humor recognition to Irony detection: The figurative language of social media. *Data and Knowledge Engineering*, 74, pp. 1-12. Doi: 10.101 6/j.datak.2012.02.005. https://www.sciencedirect .com/science/article/pii/S0169023X12000237

Robin, R. (1973). Historie et linguistique. [History and Linguistic]. Selected 21-26. Paris Armand Colin.

Rojas Malacara, E. V. (2019, Jul 17). *Una criminología para las re des sociales virtuales* [A Criminology for virtual social media]. Doctorate Thesis, San Nicolás de los Garza. Mexico. Universidad Autónoma de Nuevo León. http://eprints.uanl. mx/16 006/

Romeu Aldaya, V. (2013, Jan). Epistemología para la planeación de la comunicación y definición de los siete problemas comunicativos [Epistemology for Communication Planning and Definition of the Seven Communicative problema]. https://www. researchgate.net/publication/308911396_Epistemologia_pa

ra_la_planeacion_de_la_comuni cacion_y_definicion_de_
los_7_problemas_comunicativos/link/57f70a1508ae280dd0
bb3 c32/download. In Aguilar Edward, Andrea, Castellanos,
Cerda, Vicente & Perez-Salazar, Gabriel, Eds. (2013, Jun).
*La producción del conocimiento en las ciencias de la
comunicación y su incidencia social* [The Production of
Knowled ge in the Sciences of Communication and Its Social
Impact].

Rosas, M. C. (2012). El analfabetismo digital. [Digital Illiteraci].
ALAI. América Latina en Movimiento. https://www.alainet.
org/es/active/57191

Roser, M., Ritchie, H. & Ortiz-Ospina, E. (2019). Internet. *Our World
in Data.* Oxford, UK: University of Oxford. [Web Page]. https:
//ourworldindata.org/in ternet.

Rowan, J. (2015, Feb). Inteligencia idiota, política rara y folclore digi
tal [Idiotic intelligence, weird politics and digital folklore].
Series Memes VI, Muckraker 02, Madrid, Spain: Capitán
Swing Libros.
https://www.academia.edu/33914729/Memes_ Inte
ligencia_idiota_pol%C3%ADtica_rara_y_folclore_digital

Ruotsalainen, J. & Heinonen, S. (2015, Aug 8). Media ecology
and the future ecosystemic society. European Journal of
Futures Research, 3(9): 1-10. DOI: 10.1007/s40309-015-
0068-7. https://eujournalfuturesresearch.springeropen.com/
track/pdf/10.1007/s40309-015-0068-7.pdf

Royce, Josiah (1892). *The Spirit of Modern Philosophy: An Essay in
the Form of Lectures.* New York, NY: Houghton, Mifflin and
Company

Salajan, F., Schonwetter, D. & Cleghorn, B. (2010). Brecha digital
intergeneracional de estudiantes y profesores: ¿realidad o

ficción?. [Digital divide intergenerational students and teachers: fact or fiction?]. *Informática y educación.* 53 (3): 1393–1403. DOI: 10.1016 / j.compedu.2010.06.017 .

Sánchez-Carrero, J. & Contreras-Pulido, P. (2012). De cara al prosu midor. Emponderando a la ciudadanía 3.0 [Face the prosumer. Empowering Citizens 3.0]. *Ícono,* Revista de comunicación y tecnologías emergentes, 10(3): 63-81. **DOI:** 10.719 5/ri14.v10i3.21 0. https://www.icono14.net/ojs/index.php/ico no14/article/view/210

Sampietro, A (2016). *Emoticonos y Emojis. Análisis de su historia, difusión y uso en la comunicación digital actual* [Emoticons and Emojis. Analysis of its history, dissemination and use in today's digital communication]. PhD Thesis, Valencia, Spain: Universitat de València. https://infoling.org/repository/PhDdiss-Infoling-83-5-2016.pdf

Sample, I. (2009, Jan 21). Evolution: Charles Darwin was wrong about the tree of life. *The Guardian* newspaper [Web Page]. https://www.theguardian.com/science /2009/ jan/21/charles - darwin-evolution-species-tree-life

Sarmiento Guede, J. R., Curiel, J. E. & Antonovica, A. (2017). La co municación viral a través de los medios sociales: análisis de sus antecedentes. [Viral communication through social me- dia: analysis of its antecedents]. *Revista Latina de Comunicación Social,* 72: 69-86. http://www.revistalatinacs.org/072 paper/1154/04es.html. DOI: 10.4185/RLCS-2017-1154. https ://dialnet.unirioja.es/servlet/articulo?codigo=5822692 and http://revistalatinacs.org/072paper/1154/04en.html

Schultz, D. E. & Peltier, J. (2013). Social media's slippery slope: cha llenges, opportunities and future research directions. *Journal of Research in Interactive Marketing*, 7(2): 86-99.

Schreckinger, B. (2015, Jul 19). Trump Attacks McCain: 'I Like Peo ple Who Weren't Captured. *Politico*. http://www.politico.com/ story/2015/07/trump-attacksmccain-i-like-people-who-weren t-captured-120317.

Sebeok, T., ed. (1960). *Style in Language*. Cambridge, MA: M.I.T. Press.

Serrano-Puche, J. (2016). Internet y emociones: nuevas tendencias en un campo de investigación emergente. [Internet and Emo tions: New Trends in an Emerging Field of Research]. *Comu nicar* magazine. 46: 19-26. Doi: dx.doi.org/10.3916/C46-201 6-02. https://www.revistacomunicar.com/index.php?conteni do=detalles&numero=46&arti culo=46-2016-02

Shakeri Hossein Abad, Z., Kline, A., Sultana, M. et al. (2021). Digital public health surveillance: a systematic scoping review. *NPJ Digit. Med*. 4(41). https://doi.org/10.1038/s41746-021-00407-6 https://www.nature.com/articles/s41746-021-00407-6

Shakirovna, S. (2021, Jun 19). In many workplaces, online communi cation is now more common than face-to-face meetings. *IEL TS*. https://writing9.com/text/60cda4d5810e230011e01a18

Shannon, C. A. & Weaver, W. (1949). *The Mathematical Theory of Communication*. Urbana, IL: University of Illinois Press. Foreword by Richard E. Blahut and Bruce Hajek.

Shannon, C. A. & Weaver, W. (1963). *The mathematical theory of communication,* 10th ed. Chicago, IL: University of Illinois Press. (1949). https://monoskop.org/ images/b/be/Shannon _Claude_E_Weaver_Warren_The_Mathematical_Theory_ of _Communication_1963.pdf

Shapiro, E. (2012, Jun 5). TV: una intervención. *HuffPost TV*.

Sharpe, R., Beetham, H. & Freitas, S. (2010, Jul 2). *Repensar el aprendizaje para una era digital: cómo los estudiantes están moldeando sus propias experiencias*. [Rethinking the Learning for a Digital Age: How Students Are Shaping Their Own Experiences]. Routledge.

Shea, R. H, Scanlon, L. & Aufses, R. D. (2013). *The Language of Composition. Reading, Writing, Rhetoric*, 2nd ed. New York, NY: Bedford/St. Martin's. https://esumsnh.net/ourpages/au to/2018/8/28/45105103/The%20Language%20of%20Compo sition.pdf

Shifman, L. (2013, Apr 1). Memes in a Digital World: Reconciling with a Conceptual Troublemaker. *Journal of Computer-Mediated Communication*, 18(3): 362–377, DOI: 10.1111/jcc4. 12013. https://academic.oup.com/jcmc/article/18/3/362/406 7545

Singh, S., & Sachan, M. K. (2017). Importance and challenges of so cial media text. *International Journal of Advanced Research in Computer Science*, 8(3): 831-834.

Skovholt, K., Grønning, A., & Kankaanranta, A. (2014, July). The Communicative Functions of Emoticons in Workplace E-Mails: :-)". *Journal of Computer-Mediated Communication,* 19(4): 1-18. Doi: 10.1111/jcc4.12063. https://onlinelibrary.wi ley.com/doi/epdf/10.1111/jcc4.12063

Schmidt, J. (2011). Misunderstanding the Question: 'What is En lightenment?': Venturi, Habermas, and Foucault. *History of European Ideas*, 37(1): 43-52.

Soames, S. (2010). *Philosophy of Language*. Oxfordshire, UK: Prin ceton University Press. https://mthoyibi.files.wordpress.com/

2012/05/philosophy-of-language_prin ceton-foundations-of-contemporary-philosophy-__scott-soames-20102.pdf

Soler, Á (2020, Dec 4). Los discursos de odio en las redes sociales se han convertido en un fenómeno social y político normalizado, atentando contra derechos fundamentales. [Hate spe ech on social networks has become a normalized social and political phenomenon, violating fundamental rights]. *Mente + Ciencia.* https://www.menteyciencia.com/discursos-de-odio-en-redes-sociales-analisis-sociologico/

Solis Arredondo, C. (2018). *Usurpación de identidad digital: un estu dio comparativo de soluciones francesas, mexicanas y norteamericanas* [Digital Identity Usurpation: a comparative stu dy of French, Mexican and North American solutions]. Doctorate Thesis. Université Paris-Saclay; Université Panaméricaine (Mexico). https://tel.archives-ou vertes.fr/tel-0179744 7/document

Soto Delgado, E. A. (2021, Jun 22). Technology in Education. https://edgyyalondraproyectointegrador.blogspot.com/

Spear, J. (2007, May 25). Presentación de Josh Spear en Zeitgeist Europe 2007. [You Tube Video]. https://www.youtube.com/watch?v=l-riD8N0Dt4

Srivastava, J. (2019, Apr 29). Social Media Statistics 2019 – 178 Must-Know Stats. *Statistics*, Zariance reads. https://www.zariance. com/reads/social-media-statistics/

Stocker, R., & Bossomaier, T. (2014). *Networks in society: Links and language*. Jenny Stanford Publishing.

Such, M. (2016, Jul 17). Los emojis y el futuro del lenguaje [Emojis and the future of Language]. *Xataka, Webedia.* [Web Page].

https://www.xataka.com/moviles/los-emojis-y-el-futuro-del-lenguaje

Sullivan, M. (2018, Apr 10). Members of Congress can't possibly regulate Facebook. They don't understand it. *The Washington Post.* https://www.washingtonpost.com/lifestyle/style/members-of-congress-cant-possibly-regulate-facebook-they-dont-understand-it/2018/04/10/27fa163e-3cd1-11e8-8d53-eba0ed2371cc_story.html

Tajfel, H., & Turner, J. C. (2004). The Social Identity Theory of Intergroup Behavior. In J. T. Jost & J. Sidanius, Eds., *Key readings in social psychology. Political psychology: Key readings* (p. 276–293). Psychology Press. DOI: 10.4324 /9780203505 984-16. https://student.cc.uoc.gr/upload Fi les/%CE%923 10/Tajfel%20&%20Turner%2086_SIT_xs.pdf

Takahashi, T. T. (2016, May 10). Jóvenes japoneses y medios móvi les. Universidad de Rikkyo.

Tang, Y. & Hew, K. F. (2019). Emoticon, Emoji, and Sticker Use in Computer-Mediated Communication: A Review of Theories and Research Findings. *International Journal of Communication*, 13, 27. https://ijoc.org/index.php/ijoc/article/view/10966

Tannen, D. & Trester, A. M., Eds. (2013). *Discourse 2.0: Language and New Media.* Washington, DC: Georgetown University Press. https://repository.library.georgetown.edu/bitstreamm/hadle/10822/1044613/9781589019546_GURT_2013.pdf?se q uence=1&isAllowed=y

Tannen, D., Hamilton, H. E. & Schiffrin, D., Eds. (2015, Apr 17). *The Handbook of Discourse Analysis*, 2nd Ed, Vol. 1. DOI: 10.1002/9781118584194.

http://www.sscnet.ucla.edu/anthro/faculty/ochs/articles/Och
s_2015_Discursive_Underp innings.pdf

Thomas, M. (2011, Apr 19). Deconstruyendo los nativos digitales:
jóvenes, tecnología y nuevas alfabetizaciones. [Deconstruc
ting digital natives: young people, technology and new
literacies]. Taylor y Francis. ISBN 978-1-136-73900-2.

Thomas, N. J. T. (2014, Summer). Mental Imagery. *The Stanford
Encyclopedia of Philosophy.* Edward N. Zalta, Ed. [Web
Page]. https://plato.stanford.edu/entries/mental-imagery/

Toffler, A. (1980). *The Third Wave.* New York, NY: Bantam Books.
https://epdf.pub/the-third-wave.html

Tunbridge, N. (1995, Sep). El vaquero del ciberespacio. Compu
tadora personal australiana, p 2-4.

UNESCO (1978). *Records of the General Conference. 20th Session.*
Vol. 1. Paris: UNESCO. https://treaties.un.org/doc/source/
docs/unesco_res_5_9.2_1-E.pdf

Unplugged. (2010, Mar 6). Monitor The net generation. *The Econo
mist.* https://www.economist.com/technology-quarterly/2010/
03/06/the-net-generation-unplugged

Valdettaro, S., Ed. (2011) *McLuhan dispositivo comunicación tec
nología medios nuevas tecnología* [McLuhan Device
Communication Technology media new Technology], 1st
ed. UNR Editora. Rosario, Argentina, Editorial de la
Universidad Nacional de Rosario.
http://rephip.unr.edu.ar/handle /2133/1743

Valdettaro, S. Ed. (2011). McLuhan. Pliegues, Trazos y Escrituras-
post [Mcluhan. Folds, Strokes and Scriptures-post]. Rosario,
Argentina: Universidad Nacional de Rosario. http://es.

scribd.com/tlatl/d/76789612-eBook-McLuhan-Pliegues-Trazos-y-Escrituras-post-2

Valíková, T. (2014). *Influence of the "netspeak" on modern Internet user's language*. [on-line]. Bachelor's thesis. Moravia, Czech Republic: Palacký University Olomouc, Faculty of Education. https://theses.cz/id/a6hvp2/Valkov_-_Influen ce_of_the_ net_speak_on_modern_internet_us.pdf

Van Dijk, J. (2020). *The network society* (3rd ed.). Sage Publishing

Van Dijk, T. A. P. C. (2005, Abr-Jun). Ideología y análisis del dis curso [Ideology and Discourse Analysis] *Utopía y Praxis Latinoamericana*, Revista Internacional de Filosofía Iberoamericana y Teoría Social, 10(29), pp. 9–36. https://www.re dalyc.org/pdf/27 9/27910292.pdf and in English http://www. discursos.org/unpublished%20articles/Ideolo gy%20an%20 discourse%20analysis.htm

Van Dijk, T. A. P. C. (2006, Jun). Ideology and discourse analysis. *Journal of Political Ideologies*, 11(2): 115-140. http://www. discourses.org/OldArticles/Ideology %20and %20Discour se%20Analysis.pdf

Van Dijk, T. A. P. C. (2008). *Discourse and Context a Sociocogniti ve approach*. Cambridge, UK: Cambridge University Press. https://www.academia.edu/5345 314/ Discourse_and_Con text._Teun_A._van_Dijk

Van Dijk, T. A. P. C. (2015, Apr 17) Critical discourse studies: a So ciocognitive approach. In Tannen, Deborah, Hamilton Heidi E. & Schiffrin, Deborah. Eds. (2015, Apr 17). *The Hanbook of Discourse Analysis*, 2nd Ed, Vol. 1, Chapter 3, pp. 466-485. DOI: 10.1002/ 9781118584194. https://pdfs.semantic scholar.org/45c4/ddd471146f175e 557e93bcd669d0ac2b5 d5c.pdf?ga=2.114637700.245071895.1572780684-201657

3298. 1567977347

Vargas Garzón, J. (2016). Alfabetización Digital. Herramienta para Informar y Gestionar soluciones a Problemas en la Comunidad. Thesis, Corporación Universitaria Minuto de Dios. https://repository.uniminuto.edu/bitstream/10656/5731/1/TC _VargasGarzonJefferson_2016.pdf

Vandergriff, I. (2013). Emotive communication online: A contextual analysis of computer-mediated communication, CMC cues. *Journal of Pragmatics*, 51: 1-12. Doi: http://dx.doi.org/10.1 016/j.pragma.2013.02.008

Varnhagen, C. K., McFall, G. P., Pugh, N., Routledge, L., Sumida-MacDonald, H. & Kwong, T. E. (2010, Jul). Lol: New Language and Spelling in Instant Messaging. *Reading and Wri ting,* 23(6): 719-733. Doi: 10.1007/s11145-009-9181-y. http ://citeseerx.ist.psu.edu/viewdoc/download?doi=10.1.1.873.7 108 &rep=rep1&type=pdf

Vázquez-Cano, E., Mengual-Andrés, S. & Roig-Vila, I. (2015, Jun). Análisis lexicométrico de la especificidad de la escritura digital del adolescente en WhatsApp [Léxico metric analysis of the specificity of teenagers' digital writing in WhatsApp. *RLA. Revista de Lingüística Teórica y Aplicada,* Concepción, Chile, 53(1), I Sem. 2015: 83-105. Doi: 10.4067/S07 18-48832015000100005. http://rua.ua.es/dspace/handle/ 10045/48306?locale=en

Vélez Herrera, J. I. (2015). Influyendo en el ciberespacio con hu mor: imemes y otros fenómenos. *Estudios de Comunicación y Política*, 35, pp. 130-146. https: //www.academia.edu/ 12495960/Influyendo_en_el_ciberespacio_con_humor_ime mes_ y_ otros_fen%C3%B3menos

Venuti, L. & Baker, M. (Eds.). *The Translation Studies Reader.* Routledge, a Taylor & Francis Group. https://translationjour nal. net/images/e-Books/PDF_Files/The%20Translation%20 Studies%20Reader.pdf

Vidales Gonzáles, C. E. (2009, Jan-Jun). La relación entre la semió tica y los estudios de la comunicación: un diálogo por construir. Comunicación y Sociedad, Departamento de Estudios de la Comunicación Social. Universidad de Guadalajara, Mé xico. *Nueva Época*, 11: 37-71. http://www.scielo.org.mx/pdf/ comso/n11/n11a3.pdf

Walther, J.B. & D'Addario, K.P. (2001). The Impacts of Emoticons on Message Interpretations in Computer-Mediated Communication. *Social Science Computer Review*, 19: 324-347.Doi: 10.1177/089443930101900307

Webb, K. (2019, Sep. 16). Here's every single new emoji we're get ting this year. *Business Insider.* https://www.businessinsider. com/new-emoji-iphone-android-2019-2

Were, G. (2013). Imaging digital lives. Journal of Material Culture, 18(3): 213–222. https://doi.org/10.1177/1359183513489927. https://journals.sagepub.com/doi/pdf/10.1177/13591835134 89927

West, D. M. (2015, Mar 3). Digital divide: Improving Internet access in the developing world through affordable services and diver se content. *Center for Technology Innovation at Brookings.* https://www.brookings.edu/wp-content/uploads/2016/06/ West_Internet-Access.pdf

Wiemann, J. M. (2003). Preface. In Greene, John O. & Burleson, Brant R. (2003) *Handbook of Communication and Social*

Interaction Skills. Mahwah, New Jersey: Lawrence Erlbaum Associates, Inc., Publishers. https://ismailsunny.files.wordpress.com/2017/07/handbook-of-communication-and-social-interaction-skills.pdf

Wijeratne, S., Kiciman, E., Saggion, H. & Sheth, A., Eds. (2018, Jun 25). Proceedings of the 1st International Workshop on Emoji Understanding and Applications in Social Media (Emo ji2018), co-located with the *12th International AAAI Conferen ce on Web and Social Media* (ICWSM 2018). Stanford, CA. http://ceur-ws.org/Vol-2130/

Winberg, O. (2017, Aug 2). Insult Politics: Donald Trump, Right-Wing Populism, and Incendiary Language. *European journal of American studies* [Online], 12-2, document 4, http://journa ls.openedition.org/ejas/12132. DOI : 10.4000/ejas.12132

Worldcoo. (2014, Jul). Los consumidores esperan que las marcas se preocupen por el bien social. [Consumers expect brands to care about social good]. https://www.worldcoo.com/blog/tag/comportamiento-consumidor

Worden, R. P. (2000). Words, Memes and Language Evolution, in C. Knight, M. Studdert-Kennedy y J. R. Hurford. *The Evolutio nary Emergence of Language*. Cambridge, Cambridge University Press.

Xiaoping, X. (2008). Analysis of anomie in network propagation. *Jiangxi Social Sciences*, 7, 221-225.

Yan, H. (2015, Aug 8). Donald Trump's 'Blood' Comment about Me gyn Kelly Draws Outrage. *CNN.com*. http://edition.cnn.com/2015/08/08/politics/donald-trump-cnn-megyn-kellycomment/;

Yépez-Reyes, V. (2018). Analfabetismo digital: una barrera para las narrativas transmedia y el diálogo social al margen de la industria cultural. [Digital illiteracy: a barrier for transmedia na rratives and social dialogue outside the cultural industry]. *Razón y Palabra*, 22(2-101): 285–301. https://revistarazony palabra.org/index.php/ryp/article/view/1203

Zaphiris, P. & Ioannou, A. (2018, Jul 15-20). Tecnologías de apren dizaje y colaboración. Aprendizaje y enseñanza. *Quinta Con ferencia Internacional, LCT 2018,* HCI International 2018, Las Vegas, NV. Actas. Cham, Suiza: Springer. p 100.

Zhang, X., Yang, Q., Albaradei, S. et al. (2021). Rise and fall of the global conversation and shifting sentiments during the COVI D-19 pandemic. *Humanities and Social Sciences Communications*. Humanitarian Societe of Science Communication 8 (120). https://doi.org/10.1057/s41599-021-00798-7pande mic. https://www.nature.com/articles/s41599-021-00798-7.pdf. DOI: 10.1057/s41599-021-00798-7

Zhao et al. (2008). Identity construction on Facebook: digital empo werment in anchored relationships. *Computers in Human Be havior*, 24: 1816–1836.

Zheng, X. (2018, Jul). The Anomie and Norm of Network Language Communication. *Journal of Language Teaching and Resear ch*, 9(4): 803-808. DOI: 10.17507/jltr.09041. http://www.aca demypublication.com/issues/jltr/vol09/jltr0904.pdf

Zhu, Y. Q., & Chen, H. G. (2015). Social media and human need sa tisfaction: Implications for social media marketing. *Business Horizons*, 58(3), 335-345. DOI: 10.1016/j.bushor.2015.01.00 6. https://www.sciencedirect.com/science/article/pii/S000768 1315000075

Zilka, G. C. (2018, May 21). Why do children and adolescents consume so much Media? An examination based on self-deter mination theory. *Global Media Journal*, 16(30): 1-10.

https:// www.globalmediajournal.com/open-access/why-do-children-and-adolescents-consume-so-much-media-an-examination-based-on-selfdetermination-theory.php?aid=86961

Zloteanu, M., Harvey, N., Tuckett, D. & Livan, G. (2018). Digital Iden tity: The effect of trust and reputation information on user jud gement in the Sharing Economy. *PLoS ONE* 13(12): e02090 71: 1-18. Doi: 10.1371/journal.pone.0209071. https://journals .plos.org/plosone/article/file?type=printable&id=10.1371/jour nal.pone.02 09071

November 2021
Editorial Letra Viva©
251 Valencia Avenue, No. 253
Coral Gables, FL 33114-6901